Diversity in community:
Indigenous scholars writing

Diversity in community:
Indigenous scholars writing

Edited by Dr Mere Kēpa and Dr Cheryl Stephens

NZCER PRESS

NZCER PRESS
New Zealand Council for Educational Research
PO Box 3237
Wellington
New Zealand
www.nzcer.org.nz

© The authors 2016

ISBN 978-0-947509-42-2

A catalogue record for this book is available from the National Library
of New Zealand

Designed by Smartwork Creative Ltd

This book is dedicated to the memory of the late Emeritus Professor Ranginui Walker, Māori scholar and writer.

Contents

Glossary

Māori/English

ako: culturally preferred pedagogy

Aotearoa: New Zealand

Arikinui: Highest chief

awhi: help

haere oti atu: gone forever

hapū: sub tribe, clan

hariru: to shake hands

Hinewhaitiri: Child of Thunder

hongi: a greeting by touching noses

iwi: tribe

kaikōrero: speaker

karakia: incantation, prayer

karanga: to call [at a marae]

katakata: Māori humour, laugh

kaumātua: elderly women and men

kawa: protocol, practice,

kaupapa: collective philosophy, topic, theme

kia piki ake i ngā raruraru o te kāinga: socio-economic mediation

kōhanga reo: Māori language pre-school

kōrerorero: dialogue

kuia: elderly woman

kura kaupapa Māori: Māori language primary school

mahi: work, implement, practice

mana: prestige, authority, control, status

manaaki: take care of

manawa ora: hope

Māori, tangata whenua:
   Indigenous people of Aotearoa, New Zealand, First People

mārama: understanding

maramataka Māori: the Māori moon calendar

marae: courtyard in front of the traditional meeting house, sacred meeting place of a clan and tribe, hospitable

mātau: knowledge

mātauranga Māori: Māori knowledge

mōhio: awareness

Ngā Pae o te Māramatanga: New Zealand's Māori Centre of Research Excellence hosted by the University of Auckland

ora: well being

Pākehā: white people (settlers), English-speaking New Zealand European, foreign, non-Māori

pakeke: elder

pono: truth

pōwhiri: formal welcome [to a marae]

Rangatira: chief

raupatu: confiscation of land by the Crown

rongo: perception

ruri: ditties

taina: younger sibling/novice

tamariki: children

tangihanga: funeral process

taonga tuku iho: cultural aspiration

tauira: student

tapatahi: integrity

tautoko: support

teina: younger sibling/novice

tikanga: Māori customary values and practices

tino rangatiratanga: self determination

tuakana: older sibling

tūmanako: hope, desire

tūpāpaku: deceased person

waiata: to sing, a song

waingaromia: out of sight

wairua: spirit of the deceased

whakapapa: shared ancestry, genealogy, family tree

whakataukī: proverb where the author is unknown

whaikōrero: to make a formal speech, oratory

whakawhanaungatanga: kin relations, connections

whānau: extended family structure

whanaungatanga: relationships

whare wānanga: Māori tertiary institution

Tongan/English

fakaholofononga: to make one feel like journeying, to make a journey pleasant

fononga: movement of a group of people with a common purpose

halafononga: route, pathways

kāinga: extended families

Kaniva: Milky Way

kaungāfonongá: fellow travellers

koloa: spiritual and material wealth

loto'ofa: love

loto to'a: courage

loto faka'amanaki: hope

loto ma'u: focus

loto melino: peace

loto matala: openness

loto: heart

loto poto: wisdom of the heart

māfana: warm spirit

mālie: good, pleasing, pleasant, relating in the Spirit and with the spirits of people

'ofa: love, passion

Pālangi: New Zealand European Pākehā, non-Tongan

poto: wisdom

talaonoa: dialogue

whawhaitonu: struggles

Foreword On becoming a community of Māori scholars

Linda Tuhiwai Smith
Ngāti Pōrou and Ngāti Awa

To even begin to conceive of a community of Māori scholars is to have more than one individual who identifies as Māori and as a scholar. A community of scholars is a collective who choose to work together across many different boundaries, disciplines, institutions and experiences, based on common purpose and shared values. Two decades ago there were so few Māori in that position that I used to refer to them as the "ones": the one Māori here and the one Māori there.

The development of the first Ngā Pae o Te Māramatanga Centre of Research Excellence was a gathering of the ones and the twos of Māori scholars hiding out in the corners and on the margins of their departments and institutions. Sometimes they were hiding in more public view but were not recognised as Māori and did not work in more curriculum-focused areas such as Māori studies, Māori education or Māori health.

The situation of being one of a few Māori scholars is experienced by many other indigenous, minority group and non-traditional scholars in the higher education system. In the broader context, being alienated, feeling isolated and having to represent a whole group of people who are generally stereotyped by the academy is a lonely place. What often made the situation worse here was that universities, in particular, were the very places that defined the Māori experience, where the experts on Māori culture resided and where the authoritative voice on Māori identity, on being Māori, dwelled. This lonely place is fraught with pressures, discourses and ways of operating that constantly undermine the diverse and real expertise that many of our Māori scholars have in their own disciplinary areas. Stereotypes of Māori—not being good enough, being there because they are Māori, not being a real scholar, taking the easy route to academic achievement—are old bogeys that are always present in social discourse. Institutions of higher education have been—and, some will say, continue to be—unsafe places for a Māori with an advanced degree.

Coming together through the Ngā Pae o Te Māramatanga umbrella was not the first attempt to do such a thing, but it came at a time in 2002 when we could gather almost 60 Māori scholars. It became an exciting way to re-imagine a community where Māori scholars from diverse disciplines could come together, could participate, and could work on common goals. A community conveys a sense of belonging, of having some form of collective understanding, of working together. A community includes its elders and its young ones. Scholars, like other professional groups, have shared professional needs and aspirations, but a community of Māori scholars has added dimensions that make it more than a professional network and more than a community of practice. Māori scholars have also been committed to making a conscious and transformational difference for Māori people. They tend to carry the responsibilities of their own extended whānau and community. They may bear in their bodies and minds the legacies of the colonial experience, and they may also be driven by a desire to set things right. Not all scholars in this community are interested in politics, but they are often made aware of the politics of being Māori by being constantly washed by the negative, unfunny views of their colleagues and their students.

Through Ngā Pae o Te Māramatanga the means to become a real community received a significant boost. Focusing on developing Māori with a doctoral qualification, enhancing Māori research through funding, and developing strategies for working together in writing retreats or on research projects were the seeds for this sense of community. Interesting outcomes have emerged from these early efforts, such as an increased number of Māori with a doctorate and a number of glass ceilings being shattered as, discipline by discipline, Māori began to emerge through the doctoral and research ranks. There are genuinely trans-disciplinary collaborations, the emergence of mātauranga Māori as a body of research that transcends disciplines, dynamic leadership, and a highly engaged generation of younger scholars who have formed in this community of scholars.

In my view, a strength of Māori scholarship is its broad underpinning of a commitment to and focus on making a difference in some way for Māori in general. Our scholars come from different disciplines, perspectives and paradigms, not all of which are natural bedfellows. What makes this community work is this underpinning commitment and a respect for the legacy of our earlier scholars such as Sir Apirana Ngata and Sir Peter Buck Te Rangi Hīroa, among others, as well as the leadership of the next generation, and the next generation. This book brings some of those community of voices together.

Preface

The volume, with its focus on diversity in a scholarly community, is a valuable addition to the literature in the field of Indigenous peoples and research, which is now a legitimate concern in many disciplines. For doctoral candidates, emerging and experienced scholars writing as an art is an integral relationship in knowledge translation. This book brings together leading Māori, Indigenous and Pasifika scholars from within and outside of the academy and tribal institutions. Their contributions are an effort to comprehend the under-studied Indigenous scholars' experience of academic writing through their participation in the Māori and Indigenous Graduate Enhancement programme (MAI) and the International Indigenous Writing (IWR) retreats organised by Ngā Pae o Te Māramatanga, Aotearoa New Zealand's Māori Centre of Research Excellence (CoRE).

In the western academy, few such stories are passed on through the generations of whānau and hapū, kāinga, āiga and tribes of a Māori, Pasifika, and international Indigenous community of scholars. In this book, the purpose is to pass on stories of this diverse group becoming better writers, researchers and wise sages to the present and generations of scholars to come and who are Indigenous. These stories might be understood as quintessential—defining, in some way, of the academics, mostly from urban, English-speaking upbringings; researching and teaching in the tertiary sector.

The book is predicated on conceptions from te ao Māori, that is, whakawhiti whakaaro (dialogue), whakahihiko (inspirational, recharging), kaitiaki (care), katakata (humour), ako (teaching and learning), tika (ethics), pono (reality) tuakana/teina (senior/junior relationship), and tūmanako or manawa ora (hope). The authors (except for Linda and Graham Smith) have been given one of these ideas through which to create their narration of retreating from the mundane world. The stories are concerned with the earliest known ancestors of a writing retreat for a community of Māori, Pasifika and international Indigenous authors, MAI and IWRs. The gathering is different to, say, the classic, competitive, efficient European withdrawal by writers from the ordinary world. Since 2004, in the MAI retreats held at Hopuhopu for the PhD candidates and at Masterton, Rotorua, Raglan, Ōmapere and Taupō for the senior researchers, the writers believe they are special and round the discussion table, each evening, over all those years, they have played out their own hopes and fears, rivalries and tensions—the nature of ancient tribal life.

Mere Kēpa and Cheryl Stephens

Chapter 1
He aha te tika? What is tika?

Waiora Port

Te Aupōuri and Te Rarawa

Te mana o te kupu, te pono o te mātauranga, te wairua o te mahi.
(Integrity, wisdom, and spirituality inform a Māori ethical framework.)

He māhinga i runga i te mahi tika me te mana tangata,
me he ngākau tapa tahi.
(A commitment to act honestly, ethically and with integrity.)

Introduction

Māori have always had to work harder and achieve higher in all aspects of life to be acknowledged by the Treaty of Waitangi partner, the Crown. In spite of policies of assimilation, we have had to try to keep our language and tikanga (within which our ethics are woven) alive against overt and covert measures, particularly in education. Where has the tika/ethics of our partner been? In this chapter I review post-Treaty policies, mainly in education, and the result of these. Specifically, I consider the dual, sometimes unequal, place of Western ethical expectations that Māori scholars face in writing a doctoral thesis. Two initiatives used by Ngā Pae o te Māramatanga show how Māori action and tikanga enhance the writing of a doctoral thesis by tauira (students). He mea tika tēnei (this is ethical).

Tika

In the *English–Māori Dictionary*, tika is the word used for 'ethical', while tikanga is the word used for ethics (Ngata, 1993). The word tikanga focuses on what Mead says is "the correct way of doing something. This involves "moral judgements about appropriate ways of behaving and acting in everyday life" (Mead, 2003, p. 6). Mead continues that "tikanga helps us distinguish right from wrong in all aspects of our lives" (ibid.). I like to think of the word translated as ngā mea e pa ana ki te tika (things to do with what is right/ethical). Tika is about values and ethical aspirations that are reflected throughout our tikanga in the way we view the world. Tika is a commitment to act honestly, ethically and with integrity.

To be ethical is to be right, moral, upright, just, principled, honest, proper, virtuous, open, decent, fair and good. Ethics is defined as the rules of conduct recognised in certain limited departments of human life. It would seem, then, that all people, communities and institutions have a code of moral principles by which they live and form relationships. Many people believe there are no moral universals, only variations that exist between cultures, and that no single moral principle or judgement is generally accepted. Some see ethics as a moral map, or a framework that can be used to find a way around difficult issues, especially where there doesn't seem to be a single right answer. People of wisdom and knowledge within specific groups feel that a set of principles that can be applied to particular beliefs, and that are held important to their cultures, is necessary to live successfully.

Not surprisingly, we all tend to think and believe that our particular beliefs and moral principles are the best. These thoughts would agree with those of the Greek historian, Herodotus, who observed in the 5th century BC that societies have different customs, and that such people believed that their own society's customs were best (Evans, 1982). It would seem that in 2016 nothing has changed

In Aotearoa New Zealand Māori (the indigenous people of Aotearoa) have to continually remind our Treaty of Waitangi partner (the Crown) that Māori have a code of ethics within our tikanga (custom) that is equally important to us as that of the Crown, and which Māori must adhere to as well. Ethics was not a word that I knew as a child and I know my parents did not either. I know, though, that both Māori and Pākehā (non-Māori) children learnt, from those at home, at the marae (sacred meeting place of kin), at church, in school and at sport clubs, how to behave within these places. This continued for the children into adulthood. It would appear ethics is everywhere, and one can almost think ethics is no more than good sense. For both Māori and Pākehā, what we learn from people combined with traits we are born with help shape the people we become. Through this learning we develop standards and beliefs that help us to make decisions when challenges come up in life.

Throughout my life, because my mother was Māori and my dad was Pākehā, things have been different. The first and very important example is that my first language is English because my dad and his relations did not speak Māori as my mother and all her relations did. My mother spoke English but not as well as she spoke Māori, so why was my dad's language chosen? Was this tika for my Māori whānau (extended family)? Our ancestors had signed the Treaty of Waitangi with the British Crown in 1840 as partners and were promised, in the articles, our taonga (treasures, language, culture, land, beliefs and traditions).

The government's policy of assimilation was enforced in schools in 1867 (the Native Schools Act), and this Act meant that English was the language to be used in school. My mother, a native speaker of Māori language, went to school in Herekino, in 1917, where she was strapped for speaking Māori. In 1937, when I began at a Native School in Ahipara, in the Far North, I was not strapped for speaking only English in this Native School. The assimilation policy was almost successful in eliminating Māori language within one generation. No Māori language, tikanga, songs or stories did I hear in that Native School. Sadly, at that time I loved the school and I did not feel a loss of Māori language and culture. That was to come later

The Pākehā teachers' job in the Native Schools was to connect with Māori children and deliberately undervalue their language and culture in such a way that Pākehā dominance and fulfilment of the state's structural goal of assimilation was accomplished:

The Native School thus was intended as a structural interface between Māori culture and European culture—a site where the two cultures would be brought into an organized collision, as it were— with one culture being confronted by the other in a systematic way. (Simon & Smith, 2001, p. 3)

This goal was not without its challenges, not only from Māori but also from some Pākehā educators. Notable among the latter was an English headmaster, John Thornton, appointed to Te Aute College in 1878, where he raised the expectations of the Māori students to pass matriculation to enter university. Many of the Māori students rose to the occasion, but Thornton was told to cease teaching Euclid, Latin and algebra and to teach more technical and agricultural studies for the boys. Māori pupils were to be educated no higher than that required to be manual workers or farm labourers to assist Pākehā farmers, while the girls were to be trained as good farmers' wives or to housekeep for the Pākehā farmers' wives (Simon, 1990).

The continual fight by Māori and some liberal Pākehā for equal educational rights was heightened by the Benton research in 1979. Benton found that Māori language was in a stage of decay and was dying. In response, the kōhanga reo (Māori language nest) movement evolved and flourished (Benton, 1979). Following on from kōhanga reo, kura kaupapa Māori and bilingual classes were established in primary and secondary schools. Some iwi (tribes) established their wānanga (tribal university). Despite all this, for Māori, it is still a challenge to change, for the better, the belief held by New Zealand Pākehā society that Māori are not capable of taking part in all aspects of New Zealand society and the economy.

Māori have fought hard for equality, as promised in the Treaty of Waitangi. For the majority of Māori people equality has still not come to pass, and statistics continue to show that many Māori people are still not succeeding educationally and our health is poor. As the title of Ranginui Walker's book exhorts, Māori must, "ka whawhai tonu matou" (keep on fighting). Therefore, let us leave the late 19th and 20th centuries and look at an exciting initiative of the 21st century in which a community of scholars strives for ethical equality and excellence.

Ngā Pae o te Māramatanga

In 2002 a national Centre of Research Excellence (CoRE), hosted by the University of Auckland with funding from the government, was established. This was after a "competitive process of bidding overseen by government and one of only eight centres of research excellence in the country" (Smith, 2012, p. 134). Professor Linda Smith, a social scientist and educator, and Professor Michael Walker, an internationally acclaimed biological scientist, were appointed the CoRE's joint directors.

Professor Sir Hirini Moko Mead named the CoRE Ngā Pae o te Māramatanga, which translates as 'horizons of insights'. The name is symbolic and explains the whakataukī (proverb) about the pursuit of horizons of understanding so that people emerge into the world of light. Most recently, the CoRE has become known as Ngā Pae o te Māramatanga, New Zealand's Māori Centre of Research Excellence. Māori academics from the Universities of Auckland, Waikato, Wellington, Canterbury and Otago, Te Wānanga o Aotearoa, Te Whare Wānanga o Awanuiārangi, Auckland War Memorial Museum and Landcare worked together. The CoRE's vision is to carry out excellent research that is significant and meaningful for Māori society. Māori tauira/students in the associated institutions were offered opportunities to reach their full potential. I focus on two of these opportunities that I found to be of significant help to me.

The Māori and Indigenous (MAI) doctoral bridging and mentoring programme

This programme was designed by Professor Graham Hingangaroa Smith, of the University of Auckland, and soon spread to other universities. His vision of 500 Māori PhD graduates within 5 years was received well by all of the dominant society. The main reason for the programme was to support Māori to complete a doctoral degree. MAI united the students in tikanga Māori.

In 1996 Dr Ingrid Winship, Director of Genetic Services at Auckland Public Hospital, had approached me to consider a position to study how Māori face DNA testing in the case of a hereditary cancer. Writing the proposal for the PhD was difficult because this was a new field for me. I felt no affinity with the molecular medicine students, who were pure, not social, scientists. They tried to make me feel comfortable but I was like a fish out of water.

When I was invited to the MAI programme in 2003 I thought that my prayers had been answered. At that time I was feeling depressed and lost. I was so excited to attend my first MAI meeting in the Māori Studies Department at the University of Auckland. This had been my spiritual and cultural home in 1988, the year Waipapa Marae opened. This community of Māori scholars was so happy because, at last, the University of Auckland had validated our people and tikanga. The MAI meeting was like a homecoming for me. There were Māori students from different tribes, ages, disciplines and universities, and indigenous students from overseas. It was so reassuring to make tribal connections and to be proud to be Māori. As each scholar rose to kōrero/speak about their research, we were full of wonder at and pride in the stories, and we began to feel empowered instead of feeling alone and inadequate.

I had likened my PhD to climbing a mountain, and already I was finding the climb too steep. The thought that I would be letting down those who were encouraging and supporting me was a heavy burden to bear. Here we were able to discuss problems and often someone in the group had overcome a similar problem and was able to help. Some problems kept me awake at night, worrying about to how to deliver a paper to colleagues in the department, and at conferences in Aotearoa and overseas. We discussed this and practised our delivery at these meetings. I looked forward to the monthly meetings and the knowledge that we could email or phone our community of scholars. This gave me a great sense of support, and also a feeling that I also could be of some support. Again our tikanga of tautoko (support) and manaaki (kindness) came to the fore and we were strengthened. I would now like to present the second source of help.

The first Māori doctoral retreat at the Tainui-endowed college at Hopuhopu in 2004

Introduction
The late Sir Robert Mahuta was the adopted brother of Te Arikinui Dame Te Ātairangikaahu (the late Arikinui/Māori Queen). His dream was to establish an endowed college where future leaders of the Tainui

iwi could develop what he called intellectual power. His vision was a challenge to Tainui iwi and Waikato University academia. Te Arikinui Dame Te Ātairangikaahu opened the college on 1 February 2000. The first Ngā Pae o te Māramatanga retreat was held at the college, at Hopuhopu, from 28 January to 5 February 2004, and we were the first group to take up residence.

What do I remember about our first retreat? As I turned right off the main highway into Old Taupiri Road and drove up the hill, I gazed at wonderful poupou (carved posts) that lined the way to the courtyard. I saw an impressive architecturally designed building. To the left was the garden memorialising Sir Robert. This was unusual as the kahui ariki (elite chiefs) of Tainui are usually buried on Taupiri, their sacred mountain. I looked around and saw faces I recognised. There was Linda Smith: she called out to me and said we were to have a pōwhiri (formal welcome and greeting) and I was to be the kaikaranga (reply to the call from the tangata whenua/host group). The community of scholars gathered to be welcomed. At times like this I quietly call on my tūpuna (ancestors) to help me with the words to reply to the karanga.

The karanga from the tangata whenua calling us on as waewae tapu (first-time visitors) rang out across the sacred courtyard; we moved forward respectfully, pausing to honour the dead. We entered the foyer with its magnificent carvings and taonga displayed throughout the Western architecturally designed building. The tangata whenua welcomed us with great ceremony and proudly spoke of the history of the college and the illustrious rangatira (chief) whose dream it had been to erect it. At the end of the speeches we all were greeted with a hongi (touching of noses) and shaking of hands by the hosts, and then we proceeded to the dining room for refreshments that ended the formal welcome.

Tika

The community of scholars was delighted with the outstanding facilities provided by Tainui and wanted to learn more about this wonderful college and its whakapapa (history). We were fortunate that one of the staff members was also a doctoral candidate of Tainui descent. Her father was a member of the senior kaumātua to the Arikinui and through this connection she was asked by the directors of the CoRE to lead the organisation and preparation for the retreat. Who better than a young woman educated as a primary school teacher and later a scholar in the university and, from birth, learning the culture of her people, Waikato Tainui! She carried out all duties with warmth, enthusiasm, style and aplomb, and other doctoral candidates assisted her. Already we see in her and our attendance at the first retreat the fruition of Sir Robert's dream.

Every scholar was allotted a room with an ensuite, desk and facilities for computers. There were four pods, each with a lounge, a kitchen and dining area equipped with a refrigerator and microwave. Dinner was held in the main dining room. Special facilities for a disabled student were available. Within the community was a young mother with her baby, and her mother close by to look after the mokopuna (grandchild). The arrangement enabled the young student to take advantage of the retreat while continuing to breastfeed her child. The young mother laughed as she told me that "There even was a 'doctor, doctor' next door [meaning a medical doctor who was a PhD candidate] to look after the baby if needed" (personal communication, 2016).

As a community of scholars everyone could begin the day as they wished. Some chose an early morning run or swim, and for others there was a work-out in the gym. For me an early morning coffee and a chat followed by breakfast and then to work was tikanga. How wonderful it was to be able to work in a stress-free environment and to focus on my thesis, knowing that if any questions or problems arose I would be able to discuss these with colleagues, or make an appointment with one of the joint directors or visiting university lecturers.

From 5.30 to 6.30 pm we had drinks and nibbles before dinner. This was the only place and time that alcohol could be consumed, and we were told of these conditions. Sometimes rules are not always adhered to, and in this case a senior staff member, who was able to settle the problem amicably, approached a person who wanted an alcoholic drink other than at the happy hour, and tika was maintained. Every evening a seminar was held, led by a noted Māori scholar, business leader, policy agent or researcher. Two I remember in particular were Dr Otene Rakena, a gifted musician who was also a singer, and Dr Brett Graham, a highly talented sculptor and artist; we listened with deep interest to their lectures.

It was through the aforementioned doctoral candidate from Tainui

Waikato that we were honoured by the presence of Te Arikinui Dame Te Ātairangikaahu and her husband, Whatumoana Paki, at the memorial dinner on the third anniversary of the death of Sir Robert Mahuta. On this special night the honourable Nanaia Mahuta, MP for Waikato and a daughter of Sir Robert Mahuta, addressed us. The after-dinner speaker was Emeritus Professor Ranginui Walker, who looked back and spoke of his experiences as a writer and commentator on Māori and New Zealand issues. Indeed, we do believe our whakataukī "Te kai o te rangatira he kōrero" (The food of the rangatira is talk).

Woven throughout the tikanga of this community of scholars is the strong thread of tika. Living a bicultural life, as most Māori do, is like sitting on the join between two seats: sometimes alright but most of the time uncomfortable. Life improves a great deal when Māori become bilingual and educated beyond that of helping a farmer or his wife. In fact life can become downright enjoyable and exciting, no matter what age. Being bilingual, bicultural and educated means that Māori can choose which chair they wish to sit on and be very comfortable on either. That is tika! Tika for Māori is to walk in te ao Māori (Māori society) with pride and humility, as well as in te ao Pākehā with confidence and equity.

References

Benton, R. (1979). *Who speaks Māori in New Zealand?* Wellington: New Zealand Council for Educational Research.

Evans, J. A. S. (1982). *Herodotus.* Boston, MA: Twayne Publishers.

Mead, H. (2003). *Tikanga Māori: Living by Māori values.* Wellington: Huia Publishers.

Ngata, H. M. (1993). *English–Maori dictionary.* Wellington: Learning Media.

Simon, J. A. (1990). *The place of schooling in Māori–Pākehā relations.* IRI PhD thesis series number 1. Auckland: Te Whare Wānanga o Tāmaki Makaurau/ International Research Institute for Māori and Indigenous Education, University of Auckland.

Simon, J., & Smith, L. (Eds.). (2001). *A civilised mission?: Perceptions and representations of the New Zealand Native Schools system.* Auckland: Auckland University Press.

Smith, L. T., (2012). *Decolonising methodologies* (2nd Ed.). London & New York: Zed Books.

Chapter 2 An overview of the development of the MAI programme

Graham Hingangaroa Smith

Ngāti Porou, Ngāti Apa, Ngāti Kahungunu, Kāti Mamoe

Introduction

In this chapter I want to address the historical development of the Māori and Indigenous Graduate Enhancement programme (MAI), because this is something that is often not widely understood or appreciated. I do this not as an honorific reflection but as an example of transformative engagement and transformative outcomes within the New Zealand tertiary education sector. A key lesson here is that we (Māori) do not have to wait for other interest groups to develop us from outside: we have the power to imagine for ourselves and to self-develop in ways that can more profoundly deliver our own aspirations. In this sense, the MAI programme is an example of resistance and struggle by Māori to achieve more equitable outcomes in higher education.

A background to the MAI programme

Although the MAI programme 'materialised' in 1988, its philosophical foundations evolved much earlier. The theoretical roots of MAI are located in the kaupapa Māori theory and practice that evolved out of the kōhanga reo and kura kaupapa Māori movements that came to prominence in 1982. An important part of the original kōhanga reo revolution included significant shifts in the way that Māori communities thought about and resisted the ongoing colonisation and assimilation of Māori language, culture and knowledge. For example, increasing numbers of Māori:

- came to realise that any sustainable revolution of the Māori economic, social and cultural condition would need to be founded on a prior or simultaneous education and schooling revolution
- began to place an emphasis on self-development rather than simply 'development' of Māori communities by other external interest groups
- developed a growing realisation that the problem of high and disproportionate levels of continued educational and schooling underdevelopment was to a large extent reproduced through a colonising imperative within the nexus of state Pākehā-dominant interests, which were inherent in most education and schooling initiatives at that time.

Increasing numbers of Māori withdrew from simply engaging in singular project-oriented interventions and began to understand the critical need to engage in 360-degree (holistic) intervention. That is, there was an understanding that Māori transformative struggle needed to engage in an approach that responded to multiple needs, in multiple sites, often simultaneously. The Māori struggle for social, economic and cultural self-development needed to engage on many fronts (c.f. Antonio Gramsci's (1971) critical notions of "war of manoeuvre" and "war of position").

Increasing numbers of Māori argued for the validity and legitimacy of Māori language, knowledge and culture as an important and taken-for-granted outcome of schooling. The need to protect our people against the loss of language and culture was often advanced as the main reason to include these things within schooling. However, another important reason for the inclusion of these cultural elements was the understanding that when a learner's cultural identity is positively reinforced and reflected in the schooling system, learning is more likely to occur.[1]

Finally, following the struggle and heightened politics that accompanied the establishment of kōhanga reo and kaupapa Māori, more and more Māori became critically aware of the politics of colonisation and assimilation. As a consequence, more communities not only began to develop critical tools that could identify and analyse these issues, but also developed skills to resist and overthrow them. In this regard Māori communities have over time become more critically 'conscientised'.

In coming to appreciate the development of the MAI programme, it is also important to understand the evolution of kaupapa Māori theory. This term was first coined in my work (Smith, 1999), whereby I deliberately used and associated the notion of 'theory' with Māori language, knowledge and cultural thinking. At the time this was a direct challenge to the narrow and selected construction of what counted as significant knowledge within the Western academy. Māori knowledge at this time was often marginalised as myth, folklore and primitive thought, which was to be considered as mostly non-factual and unscientific. In other words, Māori culture, language and knowledge were diminished as not 'real' or 'authentic' knowledge. My challenge was to the narrowly defined interpretation of what was to be legitimated as 'theory' in the Western-biased academy, and, by extension, what knowledge was to be excluded and marginalised.

The critical point here is the way in which the control over what was to count as theory within the prestigious intellectual space of the academy undermined Māori cultural positioning in society. The selective marginalisation of the validity of Māori within the academy needed to be confronted as a significant site and mode of colonisation. In my PhD thesis (Smith, 1997) I drew on research work and practical experiences associated with the kōhanga reo and kura kaupapa Māori movements in the 1980s and 1990s. In particular, the study looked at Māori parents who had elected to withdraw their children from compulsory state-sponsored schooling and put them into the Māori cultural options of te kōhanga reo and kura kaupapa Māori. In this thesis I

---

1 C.f. Pierre Bourdieu's writings on social and cultural capital (Bourdieu, 1972).

identified a set of key principles[2] within these kaupapa Māori strategies which were concerned with addressing high and disproportionate
levels of Māori-language loss, in particular, and social, economic and
educational underdevelopment in general. Furthermore, I argued that
if these intervention elements could be made portable (as theory) and
then applied to other sites of Māori crisis, there would be a strong like-
lihood of reproducing the positive, transformative outcomes seen in
te kōhanga reo and kura kaupapa Māori sites. These kaupapa Māori
intervention elements were to underpin the original thinking on the
establishment, philosophy and practice of the MAI programme, which
began within the Education Department at the University of Auckland.

The origins and development of the MAI programme

The MAI programme was originally conceived and articulated as part of
the appointment process of Linda Smith and me to a joint position in the
Education Department (University of Auckland) in 1988. This 'Māori'
position was created by the Department in response to the advocacy of
a number of individuals, particularly Dr Stuart McNaughton and Dr
Alison Jones, who were the primary promoters of this position. In the
selection seminar preceding the appointment Linda and I made it clear
that if we were to be chosen we were not interested in simply adding "bits
and pieces" of Māori content to existing lectures and programmes. While
this was acknowledged as an important first step, we made it clear that
the focus of our effort would be on creating "Māori papers, courses and
degree pathways for Māori students first and foremost". Furthermore, a
significant part of our effort was to be put into growing a Māori graduate
programme of substance within the Education Department. We argued
that such an emphasis presupposed the growth of Māori student success
at the undergraduate level.

---

2 These intervention elements are:

  1. tino rangatiratanga (self-development principle)

  2. ngā taonga tuku iho (cultural aspirations principle)

  3. ako Māori (culturally preferred ways of learning principle)

  4. kia piki ake i ngā raruraru o te kainga (socioeconomic mediation principle)

  5. whānau/whanaungatanga (extended family and practices principle)

  6. kaupapa (shared, collective vision principle).

At the time of our joint appointment (0.5 each to a single lectureship position), there were only two (self-declared) Māori students enrolled in masters' programmes in the Education Department and two Māori students undertaking doctoral studies. This was in spite of there being a large number of Māori students who had majored in education at the undergraduate level. In the 4 years after our appointment, a masters' cohort in excess of 50 Māori students had been established. Once this graduate growth had been achieved, we focused on building up a cohort of Māori doctoral students in education. The number of Māori academic staff within the Education Department also began to grow exponentially, resulting from the need to support the emerging numbers of Māori graduate students. The growth in the number of Māori students and their presence within the Department also gave rise to the development of the International Research Institute for Māori and Indigenous Education.[3]

The core elements of the Māori graduate initiative within the Education Department formed the basis of the MAI programme, which was later developed across the University of Auckland through the Pro Vice-Chancellor (Māori) plan in 2000.[4] A feature of these early MAI meetings was that they were held in the meeting room of the Vice-Chancellor's suite. This not only signalled the Vice-Chancellor's and senior staff's support for the programme but also gave the programme a level of status to cut through disciplinary silos. The programme ran in this site for 2 years, facilitated by me through the Office of the Pro Vice-Chancellor (Māori). Mr Te Tuhi Robust, the Pro Vice-Chancellor (Māori) administrator, also took a lead role in co-ordinating the meetings during this time. Once the MAI group became more established, students themselves helped with organisational elements.

It was some time later that the MAI programme was inserted into the Māori-focused bid (Ngā Pae o te Māramatanga) for one of the five government-sponsored CoREs (Centres of Research Excellence).[5]

---

3 Key staff in this initiative included Graham Smith, Linda Smith, Margie Hohepa, Kuni Jenkins, Judith Simon, Stuart McNaughton, Alison Jones, Michael Peters, James Marshall, Roger Dale, and a number of senior Māori graduate students.

4 In this plan the MAI programme aimed to develop (or have in process) 500 Māori PhDs in 5 years. In reality the target took around 7 years to achieve.

5 This was in 2002; see http://www.maramatanga.co.nz

The reasoning for this was not just to broaden the success of the MAI programme to a national level; it also served the purpose of providing an ideal mechanism for a capacity-building output for Māori researcher development across the country. Moreover, it was an initiative that was already proving successful. The capacity-building output was a requirement of the first CoRE bidding process.

Some of the strategic elements of the graduate intervention programme that were originally developed within education and later reshaped into the national MAI initiative included:

- a strategic shift to focus on Māori doctoral development, the presumption being that undergraduate success and master's development were prerequisites for such an emphasis

- proactively identifying and recruiting Māori with the appropriate undergraduate degrees who had the capacity to go on to higher study at the doctoral level

- actively providing assistance to get prospective students successfully enrolled: often this called for an understanding of the students' domestic circumstances, financial circumstances and support networks, but sometimes students also needed help to select appropriate thesis topics, research subjects, supervisory support, and so on

- assistance in finding scholarship and fees opportunities

- meetings with individual students to help find specialist ongoing mentoring and support

- the provision of regular meetings (usually on Saturday mornings) of Māori graduate students as a collective cohort in which cultural sharing, knowledge sharing and general support were all significant components

- development of a set format for these Saturday meetings, with regular slots for different activities, the provision of food, and strict adherence to the time schedule so that students knew that we would finish by 2.30 pm and they could plan with certainty their days and organise family, etc. accordingly

- a major focus on building student confidence and competence with research skills, methods and methodologies, as well as supporting students who might be struggling with theoretical issues and understanding.

Another, very important, part was the instilling of collective values and responsibilities (whanaungatanga) and a consciousness of the 'politics' of Māori living (and studying) in societal and institutional contexts of unequal social and power relations.

International outreach: The Canadian SAGE programme

When I stepped down from the Pro Vice-Chancellor position at the University of Auckland to take up the Distinguished Visiting Professor in Indigenous Education appointment under the Universitas 21 collaboration, hosted by the University of British Columbia in Canada,[6] these ideas were introduced into the international arena.[7] By this time the MAI programme had become more formally entrenched within Ngā Pae o te Māramatanga, the Māori Centre of Research Excellence. As such it came under the stewardship of the co-directors of that time, Professor Linda Smith and Associate Professor Michael Walker. Once MAI came under the influence of Ngā Pae o te Māramatanga it became more formally resourced by CoRE funding, and the capacity-building outcomes became more focused as a result of the formal accountabilities associated with the receipt of government funding. A significant element that was added to the Ngā Pae o te Māramatanga programme was the establishment of a national database of Māori PhD development, which was overseen by Professor Les Williams.

I initiated the programme in British Columbia with the aid of Professor Jo-Ann Archibald and Dr Lee Brown. 'SAGE' became the acronym for the initiative of Supporting Aboriginal Graduate Enhancement. The name is significant in the native Canadian and American cultural context because sage is also a sacred plant that is important for ceremonial use. The Canadian programme was seeded at the University of British Columbia campus but very quickly spread to cover most of the doctoral granting institutions[8] across the province of

---

6 In 2001.

7 MAI was also introduced at various institutions in Australia, the US mainland and Alaska.

8 Programmes were established at the University of British Columbia, UBC Okanagan, Simon Fraser University, the University of Victoria, and the University of Northern British Columbia.

British Columbia. The project was modified (as appropriate) to the various Canadian cultural contexts in which distinctive clusters of graduate students were situated.

Like MAI, SAGE was a province-wide educational intervention that intended to quickly build a talent pool of PhD/EdD-credentialed aboriginal and indigenous scholars in British Columbia. While the MAI programme aimed to develop (or have in process) 500 Māori PhDs in 5 years,[9] the British Columbia initiative aimed to develop 250[10] First Nations and aboriginal PhDs in 5 years. Like MAI, SAGE aimed to develop a critical mass of First Nations and aboriginal intellectual talent and change-makers who would also have a strong commitment to and consciousness of being First Nations people, and who would develop skills and knowledge to contribute to First Nations development. The important point to note here is that First Nations and aboriginal populations in Canada suffer in a similar way to Māori, with high and disproportionate levels of social and economic underdevelopment when compared to dominant non-native populations.

The SAGE programme aimed to support several groups:

- aboriginal (a person of aboriginal ancestry, including Metis) students
- First Nations Canadian and international indigenous PhD/EdD students currently enrolled at any institution in BC[11]
- aboriginal and indigenous students enrolled in masters' programmes elsewhere in Canada who were intending to enrol in a PhD or EdD in British Columbia.

SAGE aimed to facilitate student enrolment and support the students' programme of study; for example, by helping students conceptualise a relevant and manageable research programme, discussing various

---

9 Simon Collins (2002, 7 March), Five year plan for 500 Māori PhDs, *NZ Herald*.

10 This number was considered by some to be a 'utopian goal' but it was aimed at many more PhD granting institutions in British Columbia than were available in New Zealand, and it was more inclusive of different cultural groups: First Nations, Metis, international indigenous students (from the USA, from the Pacific and from Africa in particular), as well as non-natives working in indigenous research domains. There were also deliberate efforts to recruit First Nations students from across Canada to undertake PhD/EdD study in British Columbia.

11 Institutions involved in the early stages included University of British Columbia, Simon Fraser University, University of Victoria, UBC Okanagan, University of Northern British Columbia, Thompson Rivers University.

enrolment options and the choice of courses and papers to augment their programme, providing assistance with issues that may arise within their disciplines, and generally building a community network of like-minded indigenous scholars. SAGE also welcomed some non-aboriginal students who had proven experience with First Nations or indigenous contexts and who were undertaking doctoral studies related to these communities of interest. Such students were expected to demonstrate that they had the ongoing support of a First Nations, aboriginal or indigenous community.

SAGE aimed to target, grow and support the development of a critical mass of aboriginal and indigenous PhD/EdD-credentialed people who would have the capacity and capability to develop wider aboriginal and indigenous development and advancement. The specific aims SAGE were similar to those of the MAI programme (although they were not exactly the same). The aims were:

- to grow a pool of 250 PhD/EdD-credentialed aboriginal and indigenous graduates by the year 2010 across the province of British Columbia to develop these graduates with a cultural and community consciousness to enable them to positively utilise their intellectual skills and talents to work for the transformation of aboriginal and indigenous communities and thereby assist intervention in the social and economic underdevelopment suffered by these communities

- to support the academic success, cultural growth and affirmation of these students by augmenting their academic work with culturally informed and supportive mentoring

- to mobilise a range of support mechanisms to assist all First Nations, aboriginal and indigenous students (and master's students who intended going on to PhD/EdD or who were bridging to PhD/EdD)—the intention has been to support all aboriginal and indigenous PhD students, irrespective of their individual institutional context, and to take a province-wide approach to this intervention

- to strategically locate mentoring pods/cohorts across the province— there were four key institutional sites: UNBC at Prince George; Okanagan College in Kelowna (shared with Thompson Rivers University at Kamloops); UBC and SFU in Vancouver City; and University of Victoria on Vancouver Island.

The SAGE mentoring pods would meet approximately every 5 weeks. Like the early New Zealand MAI programmes, these sessions were typically held on a Saturday, usually from 9 am to 3 pm. Food was always provided. A local co-ordinator took responsibility to set the meetings up, arrange the venue, initiate and maintain contact with participants, buy in the food and generally be responsible for local co-ordination. A key resource facilitator would be organised for the pod meeting, drawing on doctoral-qualified staff from the various institutions (e.g. myself, Dr Jo-ann Archibald, Dr Ethel Gardiner, Dr Michelle Stack, Dr Lee Brown, Dr Mike Evans, Dr Jeff Corntassel and Dr Todd Ormiston). These key resource people would contribute to the various pod meetings and help the co-ordinator to lead the day. These resource facilitators would change so that a pod would get exposure to different skills and expertise. This approach also ensured that individual resource people were not overworked, given that these academics were volunteering their time over and above their normal workloads.

The SAGE pods were designed to be supportive and inclusive of *all* aboriginal and indigenous students participating. The pods were expected to support, recognise and respect the many First Nations and aboriginal cultures brought into the pod circle; equally, each individual, no matter what level of cultural skill and awareness, had to be open to becoming stronger and more committed to having their work and practice to positively impact on and contribute to First Nations and indigenous development and advancement. Graduates within the pods who had particular skills were encouraged to share their expertise. This was often important in terms of providing and supporting the cultural learning environment, where different tribal languages and cultural protocols were positively reinforced. The aim was a more culturally appropriate learning environment and, ultimately, academic success that will benefit the collective needs of indigenous communities more generally.

Concluding remarks

Both the MAI and SAGE programmes create a learning environment in which the following cultural values and practices are central:

- individual contributions of knowledge will be valued by the whole group

- knowledge, wisdom and understanding ought to be shared for the benefit of the whole group
- we have a responsibility to all share and to all benefit
- our individual successes are group successes
- our cultural backgrounds are of value and significance
- our languages, knowledge and cultural practices can be an important part of our academic work and learning context
- our minds and hearts are open to all learning and wisdom
- we have a positive contribution to make
- there is a need to understand the politics of unequal power relations and how they affect indigenous learning.

A significant difference between MAI and SAGE has been the level of external recognition and support. In New Zealand, prior to Ngā Pae o te Māramatanga getting involved, MAI was mainly voluntary and there was minimal funding support from institutions or government. By contrast, in Canada funding support came from the School of Education in the first instance and later from the Vancouver Foundation and the British Columbia Ministry of Education. Because of this solid resource support, the initiative in Canada was able to engage in a number of other activities. For example, these intervention 'multipliers' built on the original PhD intervention, including:

- holding an annual province-wide conference based around PhD students and academic staff
- developing a website for SAGE with each regional pod having a home page[12]
- providing paid tutorial positions for PhD students
- beginning to build an accurate and up-to-date database of First Nations PhD development in British Columbia.
- Future planning included replicating many of the initiatives modelled by Ngā Pae o te Māramatanga, such as:
- creating a scholarship and funding source database (on the website)
- assisting graduate student participation and presentations at international conferences (individual and group opportunities)

---

12 aboriginal.ubc.ca

- the development of journal publications
- seeking more corporate sponsorships to develop reduced pricing on products for First Nations students in the programme (e.g. laptops, software programs)
- sponsoring of special interest seminars with internationally recognised indigenous scholars
- the establishment of some institutional awards for outstanding First Nations and indigenous PhD theses and contributions
- creating a provincial First Nations / indigenous PhD alumni group
- developing a writing retreats—an 8-day intensive writing opportunity for those students nearing completion of their theses.

Now both the MAI and SAGE programmes have evolved even further. There are many new champions and former members who now have their PhDs, and who are involved with and making contributions to these programmes. Some of the newer elements appearing in both Canada and New Zealand include:

- annual awards and celebratory events (formal dinners and cultural feasting)
- annual conferences (local and national)
- regular writing retreats and skills workshops
- scholarships and funding support (from tribes, external funding agencies and institutions)
- mentoring into academic positions within the academy
- mentoring into academic research and writing contributions (e.g. Performance-Based Research Fund).

Many of those who have graduated through the MAI and SAGE programmes are now working in universities and in key leadership roles. Certainly we have more well-credentialed and qualified people to apply for influential positions within the workforce, although credentials simply prepare people with leadership skills—top credentials do not automatically confer leadership. This is still the role of our communities and is a cultural accountability process that ensures the learning that has occurred in the academy is relevant and useful to the community. Herein, I believe, is the important purpose of the MAI and

SAGE programmes: not simply to create 'privatised academics' who are more interested in developing their individual career pathways and the pursuit of their own personal interests, but rather to support indigenous collective potential through the creation of a critical mass of like-minded indigenous transformers who will go out and have a positive impact on our social, economic, cultural and political wellbeing.

References

Bourdieu, P. (1977). *Outline of a theory of practice.* Cambridge, UK: Cambridge University Press.

Gramsci, A. (1971). *Selections from The prison notebooks.* Q. Hoare & G. Smith (Eds. & Trans.). London, UK: Lawrence & Wishart.

Smith, G. H. (1997). *Kaupapa Māori: Theory and praxis.* Unpublished doctoral thesis, University of Auckland.

Smith, L. T. (1999). *Decolonizing methodologies: Research and indigenous peoples.* London, UK: Zed Books.

Chapter 3 Mā te tūmanako me te manawa ora: Hope has a place in academic endeavour

Teorongonui Josie Keelan
Ngāti Porou, Ngāti Awa, Tuhoe

Introduction

Indigenous doctoral candidates and senior scholars move through levels of rongo, mōhio, mārama, matau, ora and mahi each time they engage in research and the related communication. Being part of a community engaged in the same process facilitates that movement, and the MAI Doctoral Writing Retreats and International Indigenous Writing Retreats supported by Ngā Pae o te Māramatanga have allowed that community to grow and flourish. The retreats have provided an environment in which tūmanako and manawa ora, both of which mean 'hope', are realised in meaningful ways. That hope is articulated here by considering the programme and activities of the retreats, traditional stories that place the retreats and their outputs and outcomes in an indigenous (Māori) space, and some articles to provide an additional academic viewpoint.

Te tūmanako me te manawa

When Tāne (or Tāwhaki, depending on which tribe you belong to) ascended to the heavens to seek the three baskets of knowledge, his hope, desire and want—the tūmanako and manawa ora of the title—was that on his return what was contained in those baskets would add value to people's lives. They would be able to understand why they did what they did; visualise their future and make plans for how to achieve it; know the impediments ahead and plan to overcome them; engage with that which is unseen and neither heard nor felt to enrich their progress—all of which would lead to a better life for themselves and, more importantly, for future generations. After all, although Tāne/Tāwhaki may have embarked on the challenge of seeking knowledge for personal gain, the result was that his actions enriched the lives of humankind.

The journey through the heavens was not straightforward. When each heaven was reached in the ascent—and there were 12 of them—Tāne/Tāwhaki was confronted by a task to be completed before progressing. As trite as the reference to that particular story may seem to some, in some ways one could say that undertaking research, often within their communities and then communicating that research to the public at large, is a similar undertaking for researchers as they progress in their careers, albeit perhaps not with the same kind of effect, personally or publicly. The same can be said of the doctoral candidate who embarks on a course of study and career development full of challenges, often the least of which is the academic or scholarly. The challenges include knowing when levels of understanding are reached so there is movement towards implementation into practice.

In the Māori world there is a progression from knowing to understanding, perhaps best illustrated in the whakataukī (proverb where the author is unknown):

Mā te rongo ka mōhio	Through perception comes awareness
Mā te mōhio ka mārama	Through awareness comes understanding
Mā te mārama ka matau	Through understanding comes knowledge
Mā te mātau ka ora	Through knowledge comes wellbeing

Unitec Institute of Technology would change the last line and add another to indicate that implementation, or the practice associated with that knowledge, is what is really important:

Mā te mātau ka mahi   Through knowledge comes practice

Mā te mahi ka ora   Through practice comes wellbeing

In other words, at Unitec knowledge is not just about intellectualising and theorising, or writing, but also value in practice. What good is theory, what good are models and frameworks, if they are not then put into practice, or they do not add value to the lives of people and their communities? A challenge the participants at the writing retreats constantly faced in the many conversations that took place, a challenge they put to each other, was, 'As interesting as the intellectualising is, how does our research, our conversations, make a difference? Kei hea te tūmanako me te manawa ora mō te iwi? Where is the hope for the people (in the research/writing)?

The indigenous doctoral candidate, and to a lesser extent the senior scholar, progresses through the levels of rongo, mōhio, mārama, matau, mahi and ora, each in their own time. Mahi is a consideration—although not always—of 'blue skies' research, which is more about theorising, although practice may have brought about the theorising in some cases. Certainly I have been as engaged in this kind of writing as in the next level. Each of the scholars, though, would argue that the process of arriving at a place of contemplation and writing has been as a result of mahi. However, the mahi referred to, in the addition to the whakataukī above, is about implementation, making things happen, making a difference, adding value out there beyond the academy.

The writing retreats added value through the many forms of communication that occurred both during and after them (Lambert, 2006). Those opportunities to communicate gave each person who participated the permission to explore, to put forward ideas for others to examine, to interrogate and critique. The result was a better place from which hope could be realised with and by others. Those opportunities to share, critique and interrogate during the writing retreats often resulted in more meaningful outputs: outputs of a better quality in terms of writing and thinking. They also served to strengthen the community of research practitioners, academics and scholars. Community and communication in their many forms are essential to that process, because they both enable critique to be given, received and acted upon, thereby developing thinking that is critically deepened over time—like those 'Aha!' moments when the student, researcher, scholar and academic recognise they have reached a moment of clarity in their thinking, enabling movement to the next level. It was and is community and communication that the MAI Doctoral Writing Retreats for indigenous doctoral candidates, as well as the International Indigenous Writing Retreats for senior researchers, have provided; where tūmanako and manawa ora were given space, allowed to flourish and manifested in many different ways.

Tūmanako and manawa ora both mean 'hope', but each word has other meanings. For example, tūmanako also means 'desire' and 'wish', and manawa ora, 'breath of life'. So how did the MAI Doctoral Writing Retreats for indigenous doctoral candidates, as well as the International Indigenous Writing Retreats both supported by Ngā Pae o te Māramatanga manifest these states of being? But first, why are hope, desire, wish and breath of life important in the context of writing retreats for indigenous doctoral candidates and senior researchers, scholars and academics?

An indigenous researcher, academic and scholar, no matter the space and place they occupy, is not alone. Take indigenous (Māori) women, for example. More of them undertake tertiary study than Māori men (Lambert, 2006; Ministry of Education, 2015), and with them they bring the hope, desire and wishes of their ancestors, their parents and their parents' generation, their own generation, their children's generation, and the generations that stretch out before them into infinity, long after they have joined their ancestors. It seems burdensome when stated like this, but their company is often the inspiration to keep going so that their hope, desire and wishes may be manifested through actions—actions that make a difference no matter how small and insignificant they sometimes seem. The presence of the many is the reason for the inclusion of tūmanako and manawa ora in this larger work.

The retreat

The many is also a reference to those who attended the two different writing retreats, where opportunities for indigenous doctoral candidates and senior researchers to commune were provided. The hope was always that, as a result, a community of researchers and scholars would form and begin to exchange their knowledge with each other. The hope being the exchange would counteract the potential and often the actual assumption that the prevailing knowledge is that of the West, the non-indigenous; that which privileges the White world view in particular. The hope was that the writing retreats would privilege the knowledge of the various indigenous world views, and so they did and continue to do so. Why is that important?

In the past the research, and therefore the writing about it, was done *on* indigenous people. The pivotal challenge to this came in the late 1990s with Linda Smith's seminal work *Decolonising Methodologies* (1999). This is not to say that indigenous researchers had not challenged the status quo previously; what Smith did was put that challenge into a single work that was to have a significant impact on how indigenous researchers engaged in research and how non-indigenous researchers reacted to being challenged about their work in indigenous spaces. The hope of Smith and others, for whom the writing retreats were part of a vision to grow indigenous research and researchers, was that indigenous researchers would not continue the same practice of doing research to and on their own. Rather, they would engage in research that added value to the lives of their people. An important aspect that Smith and others envisioned would add value was the writing retreats, which they thought would provide space in the lives of those researchers to articulate, in a piece of writing, what they had studied, the thinking that went with their research, and the related outputs and outcomes. The reason is that writing articles is highly valued in the world of research and academia, and articles are regarded as essential for communicating research practice. Thus the writing undertaken by the scholars at the retreats was primarily for the academic world, although sometimes accessed by a practitioner. A challenge for future retreats would be the article focused on the practitioner and their magazines as opposed to the academic journal.

The retreats were opportunities not only to produce a piece of writing but also to spend time in knowledge exchange with others. As a result of that exchange, the hope was that the networks begun decades earlier by indigenous scholars (for example, in Aotearoa by Patu Hohepa, the late Ranginui Walker, Pare Hopa, and the late Robert (Bob) Mahuta), would strengthen and grow. That hope has been realised with invitations to contribute to books, to speak at conferences in each other's countries, to co-author an article, chapter or book, to share all aspects of space and time in ways that enhance the wellbeing of each other and the different world views each brings to the conversation. The hope is that this ongoing exchange will result in a growing body of knowledge, indigenous knowledge that will be a contribution to the potential for economic, political and social development of indigenous peoples. Certainly an outcome has been an accumulation of knowledge. Whether the knowledge has been beneficial for different indigenous people is yet to be ascertained. There has been a substantial growth in the number of indigenous academics and scholars, but is that enough? Surely the hope engendered in the retreats was that eventually what would be seen was a definite improvement in the wellbeing (manawa ora) of wider indigenous peoples beyond that of the researcher, academic and scholar.

As Patu Hohepa said in the key note address in 2010, at the MAI Doctoral Writing Retreat, as part of the Manu Ao Leadership Academy:

> The message for you who are just beginning the doctoral path is not
> to lose human understanding in the search for academic knowledge
> and footholds. You can be Māori—meaning normal, ordinary; you
> can also be Māoriori, meaning free from anxiety and contented; you
> can also be the other meaning of Māori—to be clear and explicit
> and intelligible without losing humanity and understanding.
> (Hohepa, 2010)

On the advice of Hohepa, then, a Māori doctoral candidate should be infused with hope and desire for the wellbeing of indigenous peoples and the collective world. The challenge for the ongoing development of the idea of the writing retreats is to make the knowledge articulated in the works that are a product of the retreats accessible to the wider community so the subject matter of the writing is picked up, used by the many, and adds value to the lives of all people. The challenge is laid because writing retreats can be so insular. Personally, as a participant I was 'shut off' from the world and the retreat was primarily about me, even if I thought what I was producing was for the many. I was fed, supported and later gave support to others, had opportunities to converse and commune, and left feeling amazing about who I was as a researcher, academic and scholar. The community of scholars provided me with the hope to complete what I was working on. They also provided me with opportunities to learn other ways of making what I wrote known to others, albeit usually other academics. Years later I ask myself whether that is enough.

Indigenous researchers and scholars are clear about one thing: if what they are doing does not make a difference, then what is the point of the exercise? Also, in the last 10 years or so research funding in Aotearoa New Zealand has become tied to engaging with Māori, communities and industry, with the idea that such engagement will have better economic outcomes. However, sharing ideas, especially in the context of the writing that may emerge from writing retreats, is still relatively confined to the academy, with only a handful of (senior) academics and scholars being invited to share ideas, thinking and recommendations to the community at large. The hope, therefore, for the future is that the sharing of knowledge that grows out of, and has grown out of the writing retreats goes beyond those who attended such events and beyond the usual target audiences of the writing that emerges. The indigenous senior researchers who attended both types of writing retreats have to some extent done so through their teaching and contributions to public policy for example, but this is an area always open for ongoing development. Ko tērā tētahi o ngā tūmanako mō ngā rā kei mua i a mātau: a hope that may arise from future writing retreats.

Postscript

When Mere first asked me if I would write a chapter for this book, I said yes in the way of an academic, to get another output that could contribute to my PBRF rating. Then she gave me the kaupapa (topic) and my thinking was challenged. How do I take concepts like tūmanako and manawa ora and apply them in the context of writing retreats designed to grow the capability and capacity of indigenous (Māori) researchers, academics and doctoral candidates? How do I challenge myself to produce something practical, because, after all, I work in a tertiary institution that is practice focused? I began by recalling my experiences of attending the writing retreats–MAI Doctoral Writing Retreats in the mid-2000s at the Tainui Endowment College, Hopuhopu and an International Indigenous Writing Retreat in Rotorua the year of which I cannot recall. What I thought about were the conversations I had with other participants, the feeling of being in a like-minded community of scholars, researchers both established and emerging, and what I produced as a result of being there. I also considered the visible and known outcome that is the exchange of knowledge between indigenous communities of researchers worldwide, manifested at conferences, in joint research activities and publications. And behind it all is the vision of those like Graham Smith and Linda Smith, and many others in all our nations who have, through their leadership, repeatedly demonstrated what it means to engage in research that reaches beyond the academy. Ngā mihi maioha ki a rātau (eternal gratefulness).

Now to go and practice what I preach—make what I do and the example of the MAI Doctoral Writing Retreat and the International Indigenous Writing Retreat add value to the lives of the Māori and other indigenous researchers and postgraduate students at Unitec, with an underlying message that our research and writing must add value to the communities in which we move. In other words, it must be practice oriented.

References

Hohepa, P. W. (2010). Karanga Hokianga (Hokianga calls). *MAI Review*, 2(10). Retrieved from http://www.review.mai.ac.nz/index.php/MR/article/view/324/473.

Lambert, S. (2006) Maori writing retreats: Advancing Maori postgraduates. In C. Fraser & L. Ayo (Eds.), *Anchoring our practice: Perspectives, partnerships, perspectives: Proceedings of the 2006 Annual International Conference of the Association of Tertiary Learning Advisors Aotearoa/New Zealand*. Retrieved from http://files.eric.ed.gov/fulltext/ED520156.pdf#page=83

Ministry of Education. (2015). *Profile & trends 2014: Tertiary education outcomes and qualification completions*. Retrieved from http://www. educationcounts.govt.nz/__data/assets/pdf_file/0003/170148/2014-Profile-and-Trends-Tertiary-Education-Outcomes-and-Qualification-Completions. pdf.

Smith, L. T. (1999). *Decolonising methodologies: Research and indigenous peoples*. New York, NY: Zed Books.

Chapter 4 Ako: Creating Māori scholars from MAI to my—A reflective journey from student to researcher

Pauline Harris

Rongomaiwahine, Ngāti Rakaipaka, Ngāti Kahungunu

Abstract

The Māori and Indigenous Graduate Enhancement programme (MAI) doctoral retreats were designed to bring Māori doctoral candidates together to write, to share knowledge and experiences, and to foster collegiality. The retreats were part of the capacity-building programme run by Ngā Pae o te Māramatanga. Based on a collective vision, the aim and aspiration of Ngā Pae was to grow Māori academic capacity and to increase the number of Māori PhD candidates and graduates to 500 in 5 years. This number has been exceeded, and there are now new goals to increase this number further.

These programmes are developed out of a need to reduce disparities in the number of Māori PhDs and academics. Although the numbers have significantly increased, Māori are still under-represented in the PhDs being obtained compared to non-Māori. This chapter reflects back on the very first writing retreat that occurred in 2004, at Hopuhopu, and how this programme has contributed to deepening my learning and teaching experiences from a PhD student to an independent researcher and lecturer.

The writing retreat

In 2004, from the 28th of January to the 5th of February, I was privileged to attend one of the first writing retreats funded by Ngā Pae o te Māramatanga. Thirty-one Māori doctoral candidates attended the retreat, as well as two candidates who had come from their respective universities overseas, while the rest were at institutions from all around Aotearoa New Zealand. The writing retreat was hosted in the magnificent Waikato–Tainui College, Hopuhopu, near Ngāruawāhia. The college is beautiful: in fact I thought of it as palatial. The facilities are magnificent, with high ceilings, beautiful carvings, a library, and immaculate accommodation. It was, indeed, a place where we could gather in comfort to write, share stories and get to know each other.

Inspirational speakers attended and we were introduced to the entire Ngā Pae team, who were present for some or all of the time. The importance of them being present was significant, because they not only provided support in terms of advice but acted as role models to inspire us to complete our doctorates and become more. The candidates came from an array of disciplines; from my own, astrophysics, to education, to creative arts, to research about indigenous views of water. The diversity of the candidates' academic research interests is, in my opinion, one of the most powerful outcomes of these kinds of gatherings. Housed under the common umbrella of being Māori and indigenous, we gather for a kaupapa (theme) and bring to the table conversations, ideas and knowledge from a plethora of subjects, both Māori and non-Māori in origin. This opens up an opportunity for creating a multidisciplinary sharing space that is unique and that has the potential to spark ideas that can lead to knowledge creation at the forefront of research in myriad disciplines.

When I first attended the writing retreat I had my 10-month-old baby with me, Te Paea, who is now 13 years old. My mother also accompanied me so that I could engage fully with the writing retreat programme. The support that was shown to me by my fellow writers was wonderful. More than this, allowing me to bring my child and my mother is a wonderful characteristic of being Māori and an academic: the idea that a child is welcomed and not seen as a hindrance at the retreat is wonderful.

At the retreat we gathered in the evening in the lounge area and talked about research, our interests and personal topics. These evenings were where we bonded and solidified relationships that continue to the present day. At this hui (meeting) I met my cousin Dr Adreanne Ormond, who would later run the MAI programme with Professor Les Williams of Ngā Pae o te Māramatanga. She and I have formed a close friendship, as have many of the other writers who participated in the writing programme. During our sharing sessions I started to learn about research that was very different to my own. At the University of Canterbury I was an astrophysicist, studying gamma ray burst neutrinos—quite a different topic to everyone else's. Nevertheless, I found their topics extremely fascinating, thought provoking and inspiring.

These interactions are some of what the programme was centred around: providing time for whakawhanaungatanga (creating relationships), getting to know each other, talking about our research, and sharing ideas and concepts relating to our theses and what we wanted to achieve at the retreat (Williams & Lanning, 2004). At the retreat there was a range of expert people available to assist us in our writing. We were also very lucky to have a number of guest speakers, who provided us with exciting and inspirational talks. One highlight I remember vividly was a large dinner that was held in recognition of the third anniversary of the death of the Tainui leader and academic Sir Robert Mahuta. One of the distinguished guests in attendance at the dinner was Te Arikinui Dame Te Ātairangikaahu, accompanied by her husband, Whatumoana, and other kaumātua (elders). Speakers that evening included the Right Honourable Nanaia Mahuta and the distinguished Emeritus Professor Ranginui Walker (Williams & Lanning, 2004). During the entire 9 days in retreat there were so many guest speakers and it is difficult to recall them all, but I remember feeling inspired by them. Also present were the student interns, who presented their summer research projects. The summer internship programme was to create a flow-on effect of students to graduate level. The interns had the opportunity to engage and interact with the PhD students and the staff of Ngā Pae o te Māramatanga.

Before I forget to mention the most obvious component of the
retreat, the actual writing, I recall that we could write wherever we
wanted to—in the library, in the lounge, or in our rooms. At the time
I found writing challenging, not because of where I was but because
that is sometimes how it is in the PhD journey. If I was in a retreat at
Hopuhopu now, in the same environment, I'm confident I could now
write an entire paper. Significant amounts of time were put aside for
us to write, and people were available to give advice and guidance.
I remember one student, who was finishing their doctoral study and
who hardly came out of the room, working diligently to finish the
all-important thesis. Those of us who were more inclined to engage
in conversation found great solace in the fact that we were with other
Māori PhD candidates instead of the isolated silos back in our institutions. These conversations were conducted during breaks, of course.

One of the most exciting memories I have is of seeing Te Arikinui
Dame Te Ātairangikaahu arrive. I had never seen the Māori Queen in
person, and so this dinner was a very significant occasion for me. My
mother chatted to her in the hallway. I think this was very special and
something I will hold in my memory for many years to come.

The collective

Mā pango	If the chief and worker
mā whero	work together
ka oti te mahi.	then the work will be done.

I have chosen the above whakataukī to start this section. For me the
saying encapsulates the essence of working as a collective to achieve
a common goal. The capability programme comprised different components, of which the writing retreats were a part. One of the other
significant components, developed in 2002 by Professor Linda Smith,
was the Māori and Indigenous programme (MAI). The MAI programme is for the enhancement of Māori and indigenous postgraduate
students throughout Aotearoa New Zealand and abroad and was mod-
eled on a programme that was developed at the University of Auckland
in 1990 (Ngā Pae o te Māramatanga, 2016). To date there are 10 MAI
group members from various tertiary institutions around Aotearoa
New Zealand.

The aim of the capability programme was to increase the number of Māori PhDs to 500 within 5 years, a goal set in 2003. This number was surpassed, and now the new aim is to increase the number to 1,500 Māori PhDs. Sadly, mainstream education has done little to increase the number of Māori accomplishing a doctorate degree. The numbers, although growing nationally, are still low compared to those of non-Māori. Thus Māori have taken it into their own hands to develop programmes that would help us succeed. Ormond and Williams (2013) collated the number of Māori PhDs that were enrolled and how many in each year had completed their PhDs between 1994 and 2010. During this period 358 Māori completed their PhDs, with 268 of these being during the operational time of MAI. With the addition of seven international PhD candidates, the final yield for this period was 275, giving an increase of 206 percent.

Most Māori PhDs graduate with a unique set of skills, knowledge and ways of being. They offer Aotearoa New Zealand and the world not only knowledge in their respective fields but knowledge of the Māori world and a unique perspective that should be valued and supported. Although many things contribute to the achievement of these PhDs, I know for myself and from others that MAI has played a central role in the development of many, if not most, Māori PhDs, here and overseas.

Ako and kaupapa Māori

As Graham Smith has stated, "Kaupapa Māori challenges the political context of unequal power relations and associated structural impediments" (Smith, 1997, as cited by Pihama, Cram, & Walker, 2002). It is these unequal power relations that encourage Māori to develop intervention strategies to combat political and structural inequalities. These reactionary interventions lead to, among other actions, programmes that are designed as transformative initiatives to mitigate inequality and to create wellbeing for Māori in an otherwise hegemonic society.

In kaupapa Māori methodology, as outlined by Smith (1997, as cited by Pihama, Cram, & Walker, 2002), there are six key elements, which have been further developed by others. The first, tino rangatiratanga, is based on the principle of self-determination, whereby Māori have control over what they determine to be important and what they aspire to. The second, taonga tuku iho (the principle of cultural aspiration), describes how Māori knowledge is at the core of the research and that cultural ways must be adhered to. The third, ako Māori (the principle of culturally preferred pedagogy), acknowledges the unique ways in which Māori teach and learn. The fourth, kia piki ake i ngā raruraru o te kāinga (the principle of socioeconomic mediation) ensures that communities will benefit from the research in some way. The fifth principle is whānau (extended family), which acknowledges the relationships within the Māori world and the importance of how these are established and maintained. The sixth, kaupapa (the collective philosophy), ensures the research is part of the collective vision of the communities being researched.

In a kaupapa Māori context, then, the writing retreat is created from self-determination, thereby creating a space where the legitimacy of Māori research goes without question. It is designed to enhance our cultural aspirations and identity by supporting Māori research and researchers. It creates a learning environment that accounts for different socioeconomic and home difficulties, such as financial support for the retreat, allowing whānau to reside; for example, my baby, my mother and me. The whole programme creates a cultural structure that emphasises a shared and collective vision to develop and increase the number of Māori PhDs through whakawhanaungatanga, through support, advice and providing a culturally safe space where the candidates and our research thrive.

From PhD to independent researcher

The PhD journey can be a struggle: not just the research itself but the trials and tribulations associated with life. During my doctoral study I was very grateful to have a very supportive supervisor who was very interested in kaupapa Māori. Even when I told her I was pregnant she was supportive, and not long after she too had a child. We had a good professional relationship and she was my mentor as well as my friend. I think I aligned myself with people and supervisors who could engage, at least in part, with me from a Māori pedagogical framework: people who would be in a tuakana–teina (senior–novice) relationship and those who could mentor me in a holistic way. The research itself was extremely hard science, with physics theories and methodology involving computer programming and signal analysis.

During my years of study I had engaged in Māori research into Māori astronomy, but I did not understand from a theoretical perspective the meaning of kaupapa Māori theory. It was not until I went to my first writing retreat at Hopuhopu that I began to understand Māori theory and practice. It was here that I was introduced to myriad thoughts and ideas that I had not heard before, let alone comprehended. This was a turning point. At the writing retreat the candidates were surrounded by Māori academics, some of whom were starting a PhD, some nearing completion and some who were long finished. Through meeting these people I learnt about kaupapa Māori methodology, cultural issues, Māori literature, creative arts, and more. Indeed, I learned about an incredible array of topics, knowledge and methods. We listened to inspirational speakers, engaged with the Tainui iwi (tribe) and met the Māori Queen.

In essence, what I am saying is that this learning process, this ako, has been cumulative and the writing retreat has been the turning point in the way I viewed and engaged in research. This is despite the fact that I had accomplished a master's thesis in cosmology that investigated dark matter haloes in a supersymmetric inflationary model, and a PhD in gamma ray burst neutrinos in the Radio Ice Cherenkov Experiment. I had very little idea then what other types of research existed, especially in the social sciences and humanities. The situation is a stark contrast to the present day, whereby the core of my research is based on kaupapa Māori theory focusing on Māori astronomical knowledge and maramataka Māori (the Māori moon calendar). In this research I combine the skills I have obtained in physics research with my ongoing learning in mātauranga Māori (Māori knowledge) to create something new. This research is carried out through a trust I helped establish called the Society for Māori Astronomy Research and Traditions (SMART), of which I am the chair, and a project called Te Mauria Whiritoi, run out of Waikato University, with Associate Professor Rangi Matamua as the principal investigator. For me, as a researcher in an overwhelmingly Pākehā environment, what I learnt during my PhD and how I was learning was not enough. As I moved from institution to institution I realised that I needed to engage with Māori research, culture and communities. The research that I had been doing in physics was simply not enough, in terms of either knowledge or giving back to my communities. This is a common theme that many Māori scientists feel. As a result, my research interests have shifted to be more Māori science focused.

As I continued my research I was fortunate that the connections and relationships I had made at the writing retreats and with MAI gave me the opportunity to grow my knowledge in this space. A few years ago I was privileged to be a part of the research project called Te Hau Mihi Ata, led by Professor Linda Smith. This was a project investigating the interface between mātauranga Māori and science. More recently I have been working with Professor Michael Walker on a study of the Māori moon calendar. Ngā Pae o te Māramatanga has been an integral part of supporting both my and my colleagues' research into astronomical knowledge and the moon calendar. The relationships that were forged in the first writing retreat and the subsequent meetings, conferences and other interactions have been fundamental in my learning and research development.

Despite its success, there has been little support for Māori science in mainstream academia. With Māori clearly not visible in the physical sciences, this makes it difficult to move forward. Other faculties seem very interested, however, and regularly ask for guest lectures on my research, including our kaupapa Māori research approach. Although there is a serious effort by Māori and some non-Māori scientists to increase the number of Māori PhDs in the physical sciences, there is at the end of the PhD a significant problem with retention and employment.

Many Māori with a doctorate in the physical sciences wish to engage in Māori research, and although this is encouraged at a policy level within the institutions and the Tertiary Education Commission, I have seen little support at the ground level. This issue I think is significant and should be addressed in science generally. In a growing academic environment where an international community is fostered and encouraged, the Māori voice can be and is diminished within the conversation to enhance relationships outside of our waters instead of concentrating within. In a society where we see a projected population of 50 percent Māori and Pacific Islanders in 50 years' time, I pose the question: How will these children be catered for in the academic environment of the future? Are we preparing now to greet them and encourage them into the academic realm?

Closing remarks

When I graduated from Canterbury University in 2009 I was the only Māori PhD to graduate that year. I was also the first Māori candidate to graduate with a PhD in astrophysics. In a field that is significantly under-represented by Māori I have found great solace in groups that focus on the development of Māori researchers, in particular, the national programme called MAI, the Māori and Indigenous students support network run through Ngā Pae o te Māramatanga. As a student and then as a researcher who has been a member of MAI for 12 years, there is clear evidence of the success of the capability programme, which has established and fostered networks, and created an array of events such as doctoral conferences and writing retreats. I have been an advocate for the programme since my first encounters in 2004 at the writing retreat in Hopuhopu.

Since then I have engaged in many of the programmes and events that have come out of the capability programme and Ngā Pae o te Māramatanga. For the past 6 years I have been one of the co-ordinators of MAI at Victoria University of Wellington, where we have seen a large increase in the number of PhD completions by Māori scholars, many of whom were supported by our MAI programme. We have an active programme that consists of weekly writing groups, monthly hui and our own writing retreats. I am currently writing with an online writing group formed out of the last Māori doctoral conference in Dunedin via Facebook. As time goes by more innovative methods of engaging in writing will be created.

The 2004 writing retreat run by Ngā Pae o te Māramatanga gave me insights into the diversity of research that is being conducted in Aotearoa and overseas. It also solidified friendships with whānau, role models and future collaborators with whom I engage regularly. These relationship have been nurtured over many years, with continued interactions through the various events provided by Ngā Pae o te Māramatanga. Events such as doctoral conferences and local MAI meetings, as well as research involving members of Ngā Pae o te Māramatanga, have contributed to my own research aspirations. They have provided the knowledge and tools for me to research in a multidisciplinary space at the interface between science and mātauranga Māori, a space that is challenging and exciting to work in.

The journey to become a researcher, a mother and an active member of our communities has been, for me, transformative. It has been the accumulation of continuous learning and experience. We do not transform in isolation, but through the interactions with friends, whānau and colleagues, and even through the negative interactions of those who seek to oppress. It is how we take those interactions and how we choose to move forward with them that defines our future as a community of scholars.

References

Ngā Pae o te Māramatanga (2016). *About Ngā Pae o te Māramatanga*. Retrieved from http://www.maramatanga.co.nz/about/

Ormond, A., & Williams, L. R. (2013). Indigenous research capability in Aotearoa. *International Journal of Critical Indigenous Studies*, 42(1), 24–31.

Pihama, L., Cram, F., & Walker, S. (2002). Creating methodological space: A literature review of kaupapa Māori research. *Canadian Journal of Native Education*, 25(1), 30–44.

Williams, L., & Lanning, M. (2004). *Writing retreat for Māori doctoral candidates*. Ngā Pae o te Māramatanga Board Report.

Chapter 5 Tuakana–taina: A pedagogy of Māori doctoral study and research

Cheryl Stephens

Te Arawa (Ngāti Hinekura, Ngati Pikiao, Tuhourangi-Ngāti Wahiao);
Taranaki Iwi (Ngā Mahanga a Tairi, Ngāti Moeahu)

Introduction

In traditional Māori society the principle of kinship is a significant determinant for belonging to a hapū or iwi. Whakapapa is the genealogical marker determined by a mother and a father. The order of birth then determines seniority, the oldest child having the mana or status as the tuakana (older sibling) to the taina (younger sibling) (Mead, 2003, p. 42). Also, in traditional Māori society knowledge was highly valued and vital for the social, economic, political and spiritual sustenance of the whānau, hapū and iwi groupings (Lee, 2005, p. 4). The status or mana of the group was determined by the manner in which knowledge was developed, protected and practised (ibid, p. 4).

This chapter is a personal account of how the principle of tuakana–teina is used, adapted and adopted to enhance positive outcomes for both Māori doctoral students and senior Māori academics and researchers. It is about the creation of a cultural space provided by Māori with

Māori to write; to share knowledge and ideas; to enjoy each other's company, laugh and debate; and to be mentored and supported within a community of scholars.

A background

Prior to 1999 Professors Linda and Graham Smith at the University of Auckland were growing a critical community of Māori scholars in the field of education. In 1997 the International Research Institute for Māori and Indigenous Education (IRI) was established. It was composed of a multidisciplinary group of mainly Māori academics with a proven record in research. The kaupapa (theme) of IRI was to:

> conduct and disseminate research, scholarship and debate which make a positive difference to the lives of Māori and other indigenous peoples, by drawing together a group of highly skilled and respected scholars who are dedicated to quality outcomes in Māori and indigenous education. (Pihama, Smith, Taki, & Lee, 2004, p. 3)

I came to know and later work with these scholars during the development of kaupapa Māori theory, philosophy and research. Graham Smith (1997) has explained that kaupapa Māori is founded on three key themes: the validity and legitimacy of Māori language and culture are taken for granted; the survival and revival of Māori language and culture are imperative; and autonomy over our cultural wellbeing and lives is vital to Māori. In Jenny Lee's words, "kaupapa Māori, as an indigenous theoretical framework, has created a 'space' within the realm of 'research' to centre Māori epistemological constructions of the world" (Lee, 2005 p.3).

From 2002 to 2010 Ngā Pae o te Māramatanga, the Māori Centre of Research Excellence, focused on addressing disparities in Māori participation and success in tertiary education and research training. In order to reach the agreed target, a number of strategic programmes were initiated and funded by the CoRE. MAI Doctoral Retreats for Māori PhD candidates began in 2004. International Indigenous Writing Retreats for senior Māori-Indigenous academics and researchers began in 2006.

Tuakana–taina: Creating a Māori writing space

Senior academics and researchers participated in the writing retreats in a number of ways. For example, on one occasion the late Professor Ranginui Walker addressed the doctoral candidates about speaking up and speaking out! I felt privileged to be in the same room as him, let alone hearing him speak. Similarly, Sir Mason Durie took time out of his busy schedule to make a contribution to the candidates' writing and research. He spoke about Māori leadership and our role as doctoral students in growing new and further knowledge for Māori communities. Linda and Graham Smith are better known to many of us, and they are held in high regard as tuākana (senior scholars). Their contributions to this book are just one example of this regard.

The inaugural doctoral writing retreat was held at Hopuhopu, Ngāruawahia, in 2004. Sir Robert Mahuta, the founding fellow of Waikato–Tainui College for Research and Development, saw the retreats as the means to grow the next generation of Māori (academic) leaders. In this connection, the retreats were a contribution by Ngā Pae o te Māramatanga to the vision and aspiration of Mahuta for the College.

Prior to this I had left the primary school sector and entered the tertiary sector to work at Te Whare Wānanga o Awanuiārangi. I was a new staff member working in an iwi-based (tribal-based) organisation with the responsibility of preparing teachers in the primary sector. To my surprise, I was advised that as a senior academic I would have to engage in doctoral study. My initial response to the advice was one of shock and disbelief. I could not remember talking to anyone about advanced study as part of my job description and interview. What had a doctorate to do with primary schooling anyway?

My colleague and advisor had been conferred with a PhD and had a vested interest in Te Whare Wānanga o Awanuiārangi. However, I had difficulty connecting the proverbial dots: I was taina (a novice), at a number of levels, to my advisor. I was, I thought, appointed to be a teacher, a manager and a leader in the whare wānanga (Māori tertiary institution). Coping with the idea of teaching adults whom I perceived as being knowledgeable speakers of te reo Māori (the Māori language) was in contrast to my prior experience of teaching 5-year-old tamariki (children) who, in my view, saw me as a font of knowledge.

Nonetheless, I had had lectures and had written about the development of kaupapa Māori theory and approach to research in my undergraduate and postgraduate studies, and my own children were being schooled in kōhanga reo (Māori language nest) and kura kaupapa Māori (Māori language primary schooling). I was familiar also with several of the struggles by Māori in education.

At the scholarly level, Graham Smith's comment that

> the act of 'struggle' itself is seen to be an important factor in the cycle of conscientisation, resistance and praxis in not only making sense of one's life; but in also transforming it in more meaningful ways, and ultimately reclaiming it (1997, p. 25)

was encouraging to me. I was encouraged, too, by the direction from Paulo Freire in his famous text, *Pedagogy of the Oppressed*, to read the world and to come to understand the injustices that arise from diverse ways of living. Linda Smith's work was also supportive (to me) when she argued that "struggle is a tool of both social activism and theory ... struggle can be mobilised as resistance and transformation" (2012, p. 199). Personally, as a sole Māori senior teacher working in a mainstream school, I was aware of the hegemonic playmaking by my fellow senior colleagues. Based on all of these experiences I made the decision to enrol in a master's degree and later a doctorate, and "to turn the consciousness of injustice into strategies for change" (Smith, 2012, p. 199).

The Hopuhopu experience

Hopuhopu, just north of Hamilton city, was originally an army camp. The Crown returned the camp to the tribe of Waikato–Tainui as part of the latter's Treaty of Waitangi settlement. When I arrived at the camp for the doctoral writing retreat I knew, by the large stone carvings that greeted me along the driveway, I was in a Māori space. Each carved post was named for a Waikato–Tainui ancestor. I felt welcome; I felt at home. Inside the main entrance is a floor-to-ceiling carving of Waikato–Tainui history. Kaumātua (elders) and young adults from Waikato–Tainui shared their histories and stories with us. They shared their struggles and battles with successive governments over confiscated land, too. We, the participants, felt their pain. They shared their archives of historical records used in Treaty of Waitangi claims. We were privileged to share their mātauranga (knowledge).

I attended a number of writing retreats in January of each year. Initially the retreat was held over 10 days, but due to increasing costs the time to be a community of scholars was reduced to 4 days. To participate in and contribute to the community of scholars in retreat required a personal and whānau commitment. For example, I had to commit to a writing plan that detailed my goals for the retreat and, after the retreat I provided feedback through an evaluation process. Of course my whānau (extended family) were committed to 'keeping the home fires burning' during my absence.

Single-room accommodation, meals and space to think, read and write were provided to all of the scholars. Initially it took me a while to get used to being away from home and having a quiet, peaceful space to myself to ponder, think, create and write. At times I did none of those things! I'd sit at my laptop and stare at the screen hoping words of wisdom would simply pop out of my head and land on the screen. Instead, my supervisor's advice to me was to think, talk to myself or talk to a colleague just like a member of my family. I romanticised the position I was in, the sense of elitism and snobbery, and at the same time feeling a sense of being out of my depth. Then I was told, loud and clear, by one of the PhD tuākana, that I was in a position of privilege and I was to make the most of my time and the opportunity to complete the mahi (writing), to build a bridge with the other scholars and not to be so self-ish and conceited. Meanwhile, I continued thinking about the original conversation, about the idea for me to accomplish a doctoral degree. At each of the retreats there was a level of consciousness-raising and we were advised by many of the tuākana that we were the critical mass of PhD-qualified Māori in the making.

At Hopuhopu the retreat was operated in a Māori way. We greeted each other in Māori; we said karakia (incantations) to bless our food; and we looked after and showed manaaki (kindness) to the many people who came to visit this community of scholars. We didn't have to ask permission to be Māori. Our cultural values and practices were central to writing in retreat from daily living. The retreats brought together new PhDs into the research whānau. Collectively, the community represented hundreds of years of Māori knowledge, language, culture and identity, as well as Western epistemologies based on their disciplines, institutions and mātauranga.

Who were these people? There was an astrophysicist with a newborn baby; a student who was writing about Māori with disabilities and access to resourcing; a medical doctor who was completing a PhD as a requirement for her move into academia; a neuroscientist now involved in international stem cell research; a well-established Māori educationalist who had been providing advice to government agencies for many, many years; and a scientist who, I was told, wrote formulas for her PhD. She is now the chief executive officer of the organisation that works on behalf of her tribe to promote the interests and aspirations of her people everywhere.

We also had a number of Anglican ministers in pursuit of their doctorates join our research whānau. They shared their intellectual, spiritual and imaginative knowledge and mātauranga with us. They were fluent speakers of Māori, well versed in their tribal tikanga (proper conduct) and kawa (protocols), considered rangatira (chiefs) in their respective communities, and they could write eloquently in both English and Māori. One of them had a love of poetry and would share his writings with us at the end of each day. They shared their wisdom and they opened our hearts and minds to new learning. As a taina I treasured the time spent with such learned Māori people.

We were blessed by our kuia (elderly woman), who was part of the writing retreat whānau. In fact she had worked in the university sector for a number of years. She was our pakeke (elder), who taught us to follow our dreams, to make a positive contribution to our whānau, hapū (sub-tribe) and iwi (tribe). I remember her completing the final draft of her thesis at one of the retreats and then all of us celebrating with her.

The tuakana retreat: Rotorua

These retreats were for senior researchers and academics. I considered myself a novice, a fledgling researcher and academic, a taina. My fellow retreaters were seasoned researchers and academics bringing a diverse multidisciplinary experiential base to the retreat. We had a number of indigenous academics from Hawai'i, Alaska, and Canada. They provided an international and indigenous insight into their own respective communities, and we were able to share similar stories with them. We also had Māori researchers attending who were working with Māori communities in various parts of the country. The retreat was a culturally safe environment, where indigenous peoples could collectively share their own challenges within their respective institutions, countries and/or disciplines. Graham Smith's work has clarified for us that "the unequal power relations experienced must be challenged and changed" and further suggests that, "transforming the mode and the institution is not sufficient" (1997, p. 273). From that struggle, and the desire to make social change, we created a critical mass of indigenous scholars who had been affected by the historical effects of colonisation and the new forms of colonisation today. We were a 'community of scholars'. This book is our response.

The tuakana retreat: Taupō

At this retreat the writers understood that the 2015 International Indigenous Writing Retreat in Taupō was going to be the last. We wanted to commemorate all the retreats by writing a book. We wanted the book to reflect us as Māori researchers and writers. We discussed and mulled over ideas at pre-dinner gatherings, over dinner, after dinner, at times late into the night and each morning on our brisk walks. We wanted to tell our stories as Māori in a Māori way. We chose Māori concepts as the theme for each chapter and discussed the idea with prospective writers. By the end of the retreat we had assigned chapters and themes (including the foreword) to the respective authors. This is the true essence of the many writing retreats over the years: the ability to support collective potential through the development of a critical mass of Māori and indigenous tuakana and taina working positively to transform our communities. We are a community of scholars.

References

Freire, P. (1993). *Pedagogy of the oppressed*. (Revised). Harmondsworth, UK: Penguin Books.

Lee, J. (2005). *Māori cultural regeneration: Pūrākau as pedagogy.* Paper presented at Centre for Research in Lifelong Learning International Conference, Stirling, Scotland.

Mead, H. (2003). *Tikanga Māori: Living by Māori values.* Wellington: Huia Publishers.

Pihama, L., Smith, K., Taki, M., & Lee, J. (2004). *A literature review on kaupapa Māori and Māori education pedagogy.* Auckland: International Research Institute Māori and Indigenous Education (IRI), University of Auckland.

Smith, G. H. (1997). *The development of kaupapa Māori: Theory and praxis.* Unpublished doctoral thesis, University of Auckland.

Smith, L. T. (2012). *Decolonizing methodologies: Research and indigenous peoples* (2nd ed.). London, UK: Zed Books.

Chapter 6 Pono and a 'write' retreat

Mere Kēpa

Ngāi Tahuhu, Ngāti Whātua, Ngāpuhi, Ngāi Tūhoe, Te Whakatōhea,
Te Whānau ā Rutaia

Introduction

Writing is an art, so how might a conception of a more satisfying or
'write' retreat for a community of scholars encourage a clearer idea of
how indigenous languages, cultures and knowledge can enhance education through high-quality writing and research that extend theory
and practice? In this chapter I will answer this question by considering
ways that indigenous scholars might work together to make writing, as
an art, as common and acceptable as writing an email or a tweet. By
considering the spirit of pono and the conception of a 'write' retreat to
create goodwill and to silence critics of passion, I will provide readers
with ideas and approaches to establish a sanctuary of belonging and
inclusion in which indigenous scholars might write words of truth and
beauty in peace and tranquillity.

Setting the scene

From 2006 to 2015 Ngā Pae o te Māramatanga, the Māori Centre of
Research Excellence, hosted by the University of Auckland, Aotearoa
New Zealand, convened a writing retreat where a community of

scholars could say goodbye to timetables, mark sheets, examinations and the daily dispiriting struggle in the academy, and say hello to a place of protection in which to talk, discuss, agree and write brilliantly—twice a year. I will discuss this conception of a community of Māori and international indigenous writers who are rising from our different homelands to broaden and deepen the spirit of pono, or authentic national voice, in education, research, theory and practice.

In Māori language and culture, the word *pono* refers to love, beauty, authenticity, light and truth. This pono is a spirit of immaculate love and perpetual light, emanating from within people—our battles, our superstitions, and from our mystical insights and knowledges, intensifying and enhancing our sense of satisfaction and happiness. Pono is about satisfaction, goodness, vitality and living, and not about fear, supine seclusion and pessimism. Principally, no distinction is made between satisfaction and goodness or words of truth.

Writing, as an art, is all about pono, which is why I will ponder the spirit, as well as praising the principle, that embraces this knot of scholars who teach and, importantly, conduct research with indigenous communities. The topics covered include being confronted with the knowledge that the university may be a dispiriting and lonely place for these scholars. In the university, Māori language and culture are not revered and our tribal histories are unclear. Māori scholars are confronted with policies that disadvantage us. There is a lack of qualified, knowledgeable people and funding to conduct research with indigenous communities, and few like-minded people surround the scholars with whom to dialogue, to regain a spirit of satisfaction and a sense of vitality. We are human beings, after all, with a purpose in life: to write to change all of this dissatisfaction through theory and practice.

I want to begin my observation of the topics that already breach the spirit of pono by referring to a visit to a zoo. This reflection will be followed by looking at topics that, instead, lead to write retreats in which we can learn to unlearn, to realise ancestral knowledges and wisdoms that are already present. The purpose of these considerations is to encourage a clearer idea of Māori and indigenous peoples' knowledges, and to conceptualise a more satisfying sanctuary in which to understand approaches through which our languages and cultures can enhance education, through writing, to extend theory and practice.

Already breaching pono

Metaphorically, pono may be likened, already, to dispirited, lonely animals in a zoo. When I visited the zoo recently I noticed that the animals looked even lonelier than they did on my last visit a decade or more before. More than loneliness haunts their spirit; the animals have no purpose in life, nothing at all to do with their bodies (Guo, 2004) and no spirit of pono. Take the lions; the moment they are hungry their zookeepers fling hunks of raw meat or pre-prepared foodstuffs into their man-made homes. The custodians seem to think that letting wild animals go hungry is unsafe, particularly when there are small children about, so the animals have become used to relying on handouts from the keepers and, of course, visitors want to be entertained by these creatures. These beasts of beauty have forgotten that their ancestors were once hunters, roaming free of people. Now they live in surroundings planned for them by scientists, engineers and architects and never have to take responsibility for themselves.

In hot weather or in cold, the animal keepers are always there to manipulate the temperature to a comfortable setting. In the zoo there is no competition and no survival of the fittest, merely a man-made facility in which all the animals are performing a role, albeit rather reluctantly, of a domesticated plaything, a puppet to be fed and put on display. Although the lions are surrounded by an elaborately artificial-natural, chlorine-scented river and pond, outcrops of rocks and exotic trees transported from the plant nursery, they seem to have no idea what to do with their lives. They wait within the confines of their respective, differently constructed, homes. Now and then an animal will utter a melancholic roar, though at other times they are not even interested in rallying a growl. The animals merely stare with somnolent eyes at the paying spectators around them. This lonely, dispiriting context afflicts all the animals in the zoo with a serious case of supine seclusion.

In less comatose moments the zoo seems to regain a spirit of pono and a sense of vitality. Animal voices rise and fall, as if the din was a baton being passed from one barred enclosure to the next in some zoo-wide relay race. The sense of vitality begins with the lions, pacing proudly through their home, roaring. When the lions finish, the tigers take their turn. Their roaring communicates to the water animals so that soon the entire pond is seething with announcements and activity. Even the birds in their grove respond by prancing about and unfurling their colourful feathers. In the zoo, in the midst of animal commotion, a strong sense of change and belonging to this place begins.

Embracing pono instead

Philosophers commonly praise the solitary life, but a write retreat for a community of indigenous scholars should be a change from the cage to a home-like atmosphere, closeness imbued with some longed-for sense of belonging. In this kind of retreat the most natural of human activities—to embrace in greeting, to touch in sympathy, to put our arms around others in comfort—is permissible (Grace, 1970). The scholars should feel a surge of pure emotion, a sense of rightness returning. Some may feel the gods, and others may see the rational working of the creation of the gods. All of us, though, should feel a change beginning to take place to the cage of anger, fatigue, fear and pain.

Māori culture ignores the lecturing moralists who have prohibited ordinary physical responses and who put in their place a frosty morality of the northern latitudes (Gurewitsch, 2002). In the write retreat there are people we know and people to meet, bringing with them their languages and cultures, their thoughts and words, their greetings and songs, and their wit. Children play among us. The men are allowed to be dispassionate and to talk about their feelings because the role of Māori men is no longer clear and they don't have to conform to the straitjacket of northern masculine identity. They are people in the same way that the Māori women are people. The women's conversation may be more subjective, because we talk about people's feelings and responses in and outside the academy. Men may talk about intimacy too. They may talk to their colleagues, both men and women, about their feelings. As educated, sophisticated, deeply insightful men and women, with a broad outlook into education, why should we discriminate against each other in the write retreat? Better that we shape the sanctuary around us to admire the accomplishments of the scholars, both men and women, and to include partners and young children. This honourable, respectful and inclusive conduct should be encouraged by all of us.

In listening avidly to each other's research and issues, and entrusting each other with our thoughts and a lively interest in our work, our loyalty to and affection for each other should not be forbidden. Each scholar's thoughts and words should satisfy the others' sense of inclusion. For a week this community should feel a strong sense of delight in belonging to this community in retreat. Throughout these days this is our place, our home, and this knot of people are no longer strangers but are bound in a community of place, sharers in mystical insights, knowledges, writing that will be relevant for generations to come. This is a fair exchange and preferable to the solitary life.

Pono and a 'write' retreat

Seventeen International Indigenous Writing Retreats have been funded by Ngā Pae o te Māramatanga since 2006 (Manu'atu et al., 2014). The first retreat was held at Solway Hotel, Masterton. The most recent sanctuary was held in September 2015 at Huka Falls Resort, Tauponui ā Tia. People from all over the world have been invited to take part in all of the retreats. There have been scholars that all of the retreaters knew, as well as new people to meet, bringing with them their language, their research projects, their special knowledge, their wit, their distinctive prolonged greetings and manner of leave-taking. The retreat is always full of life and activity as people begin to talk, to dialogue, to agree and to write about their research interest, theory and practice.

The retreaters come from diverse disciplines including education, Māori studies, indigenous studies, anthropology, psychology, sociology, gerontology, public health, medicine and geology. They come from academic institutions located in Auckland, Hamilton, Whakatāne, Palmerston North, Whanganui, Wellington, Canterbury and Otago; from the Kingdom of Tonga, Nepal, India, China, Canada and the USA. All bring collective values on research and education to the sanctuary of scholarship and dialogue. The 7-to-8-day retreats are held twice yearly: in winter at Masterton, in winter and summer in Ōmapere, except for December 2011 when the retreats were held in winter and summer in Rotorua, then at Raglan in the summer of 2012 and in winter at Tauponui ā Tia in 2015. Every day the retreaters are engaged in contemplating and writing scholarly articles, chapters in books, books, submissions, research proposals, essays, reviews, technical reports, funding applications and cultural reports. They discuss, at length, areas of shared research interest with new colleagues, and share texts and ideas in a particular research area with old colleagues. The seminars, held every evening, are co-operative attempts through dialogue without end to share answers to common problems of frustration, irritation, anxiety, alienation, despair and anger at research and life in the academy.

At the 2012 retreat in Raglan the purpose—to write and to dialogue with other senior researchers—underwent a change to include training a small number of doctoral candidates and postdoctoral fellows, and some of the Māori scholars discussed community-based research projects with their principal investigators. A few of the retreaters arrived, at intervals, throughout the sanctuary, stayed for a short period and departed. Having the university of a scholar close to the retreat added to the sense of coming and going. These people's movements disturbed the sense of belonging and inclusion—both strong features of the earlier retreats. The presence of young children and wives or partners was a new direction, and the practice would be continued in the retreats to come. Traditionally their inclusion is understood in terms of the important Māori link of whakapapa (shared ancestry).

At Taupōnui a Tia the community of scholars, although small in comparison to the 16 previous retreats, was very successful because seven of us had attended most of the other retreats. The scholars were published (some widely), most of us were well known to each other, and we were all Māori. We were freed from fear to share our ideas, experience and knowledge about our fields of research, both to our own benefit and to the learning of the three doctoral candidates attending the particular retreat.

A notable feature of the retreat was that most of the scholars were more or less disabled by exhaustion and lassitude on arrival due to the dispiriting struggles we had all confronted in our places of work. The antidote was the spirit of pono. At the end of the sanctuary, when we returned to our participation in the New Zealand economy, the good company, conversation and food, walking and jogging and the bracing winter air in Taupōnui a Tia, had dissipated our condition of over-tiredness. The satisfying feature of the retreat was that, once again, a community of scholars agreed that our workplaces were toxic to Māori. Satisfactorily, one of the professors among us was able to shed a little light on the 'new' Centre of Research Excellence (Māori), but most of the scholars clearly remained in the dark about the research possibilities and structures to come.

Personally, sharing living space with a colleague from a tribal university (wānanga) included exciting conversations about what led to our resignations from our respective education institutions and what is happening in our lives, now, as public academics. These conversations led to a discussion of projects in which we might share our thoughts and experience of research and the retreats. That is why we produced the proposal for this book.

Turning back to 2008, the fifth International Indigenous Writing Retreat for senior scholars, writers and researchers was held at the Quality Resort Heritage, Rotorua from 13 to 19 June. In that year the community of scholars from New Zealand and international universities, wānanga, health agencies, Crown research institutes and independent Māori-owned research institutes working in quantitative and qualitative studies all retreated together. This sanctuary provided an international forum for research and practice across disciplines and interests through writing and round-table discussions, as well as opening up interactive network relations.

At the 6-day retreat the scholars wrote on an array of topics, with a particular focus on their own research interest. Discussions in the evening took place on the role of the retreat in the overall responsibility of Ngā Pae o te Māramatanga to promote research excellence in terms of developing and advancing Māori in the New Zealand and global economy. This winter retreat was thought provoking and relevant, and there was an inspirational and robust line-up of chairs to preside over the round-table discussions about personal writing plans, the publication process and, specifically, about *AlterNative: An International Journal of Indigenous Peoples*. Indeed, two members of *AlterNative*'s editorial committee met with four scholars from the Ho'okulāiwi Centre, University of Hawai'i, Manoa, attending the retreat. The committee members agreed to publish 12 native Hawaiian scholars' articles on the condition that they provide an account of cutting-edge research of interest to teachers, researchers and policy makers to enable a fresh and informed native Hawai'ian perspective on revitalising Hawaiian language and culture. Importantly, the supplement provided a medium for the native Hawaiian scholars to publish political matters in theory and practice. Of course the best way to enhance education through high-quality writing is to establish an international journal. Formerly known as *AlterNative: A Journal of Indigenous Scholarship*, and now *AlterNative: A Journal of Indigenous Peoples*, the journal has swiftly gained momentum as a formidable international research publication to authenticate research by Māori, Indigenous and Pasifika scholars.

Obviously the idea behind these retreats has been broader than merely to provide a solitary place for writing. Their function has been to enable a community of scholars to inform, to explain and to communicate ideas, to create new ways of carrying out research by and with Indigenous peoples, to amuse, to entertain, to persuade, to rouse emotions, to communicate deep emotional experiences and to provide know-how. For the scholars, the retreats are an intimate contemplation of complexities, potentialities and important relationships, which we all interact with in everyday life. There is no doubt, after my participation in 16 retreats, that the scholars have written papers about their research undertaken in the field. The importance of the publication will vary from person to person. Without doubt the sanctuaries have become a highly anticipated event in the Ngā Pae o te Māramatanga calendar, in which Māori and Indigenous scholars observe, contemplate and dialogue about what remains of our knowledges, writing together and individually about what happens in our research and institutions.

What will endure of these principles and functions as the retreat is changed from a temporary to a long-term programme? Conceptually, a community of Māori and Indigenous peoples from institutions of education would be enabled to interact with each other in peace and harmony, to enhance relationships begun in previous retreats, and to engage nightly in intellectual debate that excites and encourages scholars to extend theory and practice through writing. In a write retreat, scholars would enter a tolerant and tranquil place where the ancient spirit of pono would surely prevail. Significantly, this intangible quality of spiritual tranquillity springing from a fundamental trust in people's goodwill and creativity to write would continue. To describe a write retreat as being an example of a diverse community of scholars will come to seem trite.

As I bring this discussion of a conception of a write retreat as devotional practice to an end, I am confident that this kind of sanctuary stems from a community of scholars' faith in a spirit of pono, and writers' effort to feel, to talk, to dialogue and to agree about people's research interests and life in the academy. Taken as a whole, I understand that a spirit of pono relates ideas, cultures and knowledges, and that a write retreat is spiritful and priceless; moral and ethical; demanding and of benefit to the scholars, to the tribe, to the nation, and to the global economy to determine what happens next in education, research, theory and practice.

Figure 1:
The late Ranginui Walker in conversation with Helen Taiaroa.

References

Grace, P. (2004). *Tu*. Auckland: Penguin Books.

Guo, X. (2004). *Village of stone*. London, UK: Random House.

Gurewitsch, E. P. (2002). *Kindred souls: The friendship of Eleanor Roosevelt and David Gurewitsch*. New York, NY: St Martin's Press.

Manu'atu, L., Kēpa, M., Taione, M., & Pepe, M. (2014) *Taulangi & Ngā Pae o Te Māramatanga: Collective wisdoms connecting education to peace*. Retrieved from http://www.aare.edu.au/publications-database.php

Chapter 7 Fakakoloa he kaungāfonongá: A Tongan perspective of Ngā Pae o te Māramatanga international writing retreats

Dr Linitā Manuʻatu

Ha'apai, Niua Fo'ou, ʻEua.

Introduction

This chapter is a spiritual and heart-felt reflection by a Tongan academic who has participated in a number of the Ngā Pae o te Māramatanga international writing retreats held in Rotorua and Ōmapere, New Zealand. In this reflection, fononga (movement of a group of people with a common purpose) and the derivations kaungāfonongá (fellow travellers), halafononga (route, pathways) and fakaholofononga (that which makes one feel like journeying, or that which makes the journey pleasant) are drawn upon to conceptualise the wisdom I experienced and gained from the retreats, and to discuss their usefulness to Tongan people's learning and living in Aotearoa New Zealand.

The Tongan perspective presented here is part of a work in progress, by me, to document ideas and practices used in Tongan language and culture in the area of early learning and community relationships. The ideas and practices are drawn from learning at the cultural interface, together with my insights into Tongan language and culture and as a Tongan woman living away from the Kingdom of Tonga. All of these are analysed critically for a spirit and wisdom to inform ways of enriching Tongan people's place of stay in Aotearoa New Zealand.

A beginning in Aotearoa New Zealand through continued education

My education began in the Kingdom of Tonga. Then in January 1979 I boarded a flight to Auckland and headed north to Wellsford for continued education, as stated in my visa. In the Tongan language my parents, siblings and kāinga (extended family) had already talked about my departure for continued education as "He ko e anga ia 'etau fonongá: 'e ō 'a e fānaú 'o hoko atu 'enau feinga akó". (This is how our way of living turns out to be: our children will go away to continue their education.) This statement reflects a kind of thinking by Tongans that people will be constantly moving away. As much as families wish to stay together for as long as they can, continued education abroad entered the kingdom like a powerful wave, uprooting people over generations in ways that the people have never quite been prepared for. Most Tongan migrants liken New Zealand to the Promised Land in the Old Testament (Manu'atu, 2016) and perceive their relocation as a halafononga (decided ways or pathways), and as a God-sent opportunity. Others regret the early separation from the homeland and kāinga ever since the door of immigration to New Zealand was opened to the nation.

In this chapter, a Tongan concept, fononga, is used to hinge my discussion and analysis of the koloa of the Ngā Pae o te Māramatanga international writing retreats from a Tongan migrant's perspective. The term *koloa* refers to a spirit of 'ofa (aroha, love) filling the heart through communion, fellowship, and moral and spiritual comradeship. Conceptually, fononga is a concept that implies a large number of people who are moving a considerable distance either by walking or sailing a journey. All fononga are purposeful—ways and insights to understand people and their collective values, beliefs, challenges and unknowns that often occur during a journey. Usually, the unknowns in a fononga are more valued than anyone ever thinks or anticipates, since the unknowns require fresh, renewed spirit in the relationship as well as new knowledge.

The derivations of fononga (e.g. halafononga, the decided ways or pathways of the journey) are also drawn upon to unpack ideas. The term *halafononga* further contextualises meanings that are associated with the group when they embark on their journey. Linked to hala-fononga is the term *fakaholofononga*, which refers to what makes the journey pleasant. The stars of the Kaniva, the Milky Way, provided guidance for our ancestors and navigators on the great journeys they conducted around the Pacific and beyond. Speaking about a migratory journey in education today would be a kind of fononga that requires clear halafononga—ways to learn and understand the make-up and struggles of the relationships created in the journey.

Kaniva can be likened to a guide: the broad spectrum of the Milky Way would certainly offer breadth as well as depth to the kinds of knowledge and insights required by migrants (such as me) to come to know Tongan ways, those of the indigenous peoples, and Pālangi/Pākeha in Aotearoa New Zealand. Yes, there are ancestors and spirits that travel with us and make the journey pleasant and worthwhile. In Tongan knowledge these people are known as fakaholofononga.

When I started at the University of Auckland I used to live in an inner-city suburb that was about 5 minutes, by car, from the institution. The intellectual route to understanding the university culture, New Zealand knowledge and society was much longer and more winding, with cross-roads that take a good number of years to figure out. In hindsight I realise that the struggles I have experienced and the new struggles that continue today are to do with colonisation, which overlays my understanding of the Tongan koloa (spirit of 'ofa filling the heart through communion, fellowship or moral and spiritual comradeship) that I knew from my homeland. I did not really understand the attitude(s) of Aotearoa New Zealand society towards Tongan migrants and their descendants who are now making this country their home. Nor did I understand the significance of Te Tiriti o Waitangi to Pacific migrants.

If I had known half of what I know now I would have done a lot of things differently. Perhaps things were not meant to be. However,

I have learned from the struggles of living in Aotearoa New Zealand; for example, that our Tongan koloa are irreplaceable, and if koloa, as a concept and custom, continues to be devalued and undermined because Tongans and Aotearoa New Zealand society do not understand their significance in our lives and generations to come, then we ought to open our eyes, raise our consciousness and engage in the struggles in our halafononga—to know our hearts and desires so that we can change our thinking and ways of being and doing.

Living, studying and working in education in New Zealand, for me, is a halafononga that requires book knowledge and insider knowledge, such as contextual knowledge (insights and experience) of people who know the politics of education from privileged and marginalised standpoints. Māori people and Māori academics have certainly acted as fakaholofononga for Pasifika migrants in the field of education. I have highlighted the insights and experience of Māori academics in education because they talk from both a privileged position and a marginalised standpoint, something that we from the Pacific have to learn from. Pacific people can certainly learn about Aotearoa New Zealand society from the lives and lived experiences of Māori people—their voices, struggles and loss are to be understood in their terms, and through their spirits and stories. What I am saying is that Pacific peoples—Tongan people, for example— can gain deeper knowledge about the politics of Pālangi/Pākehā education from Māori people because Māori have lived with Pākehā for over 175 years, side by side.

I consider my participation and experience in the Ngā Pae o te Māramatanga international writing retreats over the last 5 years to be one of many halafononga in which to conceptualise the spiritual koloa in inter-cultural relationships between Māori, international indigenous and Pasifika scholars. I would argue that the spiritual koloa in my loto (heart) is central to deepening the conceptualisation of Tongan ideas that are useful in developing my career and work in the field of education.

Finding a way to speak about my lived experience as I began my university education is an example of unpacking the concept of fononga in education in the New Zealand context. Fononga, as a concept, is complex and provides the kinds of social relationships that form the basis for analysis of what it means for Tongan migrants to live well at the cultural interface in New Zealand. In a sense, living Tongan language and culture is about fononga with Tongan people in the world and what makes sense to us in theory and in practice.

In Aotearoa New Zealand there are theories about, but little theorising by, Pasifika migrants in education

Since I migrated to Aotearoa New Zealand, Bourdieu's (1972) theory of cultural capital has been debated in the university as part of theorising educating Māori and migrants from the Pacific Islands. In the 21st century the migrants from the Pacific still run with the cultural capital theory and somehow they are still hesitant, perhaps unwilling to look to their own language and culture for insights and ideas. The supervisor of my doctoral study advised me that the issue with Pacific peoples is that they haven't done the intellectual work in the university yet. That is, we haven't thought about our own ideas; rather we take what they (Pālangi) have thought about and make it ours. I dwelt on this conversation for some time, and I asked myself, What ought I to think about in my own research that I may contribute from a standpoint that is original and not a variation of the same ideas that Pālangi have put forth in the academy as the truth?

In reflecting on my fononga in education, I realise that over the years of working in the secondary sector, and later in the university, I did not look to Tongan language and culture for ideas. I tried to read books with flash titles to see what Pālangi said. Of many colleagues, the one who has kept telling me to look to Tongan language and culture is my Māori colleague. Ever since I started working with her in the 1980s in the secondary school sector she would tell me to write the introduction to my public speeches and conference papers in Tongan. I did not quite understand the politics of that act at the time; I just did so because I knew she knew a lot more about education in Aotearoa and how to work among Pālangi. I was not wrong. In hindsight I realise my Māori colleague knew the struggles of the colonised and the colonisers more than I ever thought. She would always ask me, what would I say as a Tongan? What is there in my Tongan language and culture to provide ideas?

She insisted, because I am a fluent speaker and a competent user of Tongan language and culture, but I did not draw upon my cultural strength. She herself is not a fluent user of Māori, but she is a competent user and writer of English, a skill that I did not know and have been struggling with. There was something important I had never thought about or experienced, and that is what life is like to speak none or little of a person's mother tongue. I did not fully understand the value of Tongan language and culture for me in Aotearoa New Zealand society, which provide me with the very context within which to engage and deepen the intellectual work that my supervisor had spoken about. Why hadn't I realised my value and koloa?

Paulo Freire would have called my dilemma oppression. I did not know that I was so colonised. Now that the situation is named I can change and think my own thinking, critique ideas through fononga, and rethink with people who are my kaungāfonongá (colleagues, fellow travellers) and those who have paved the halafononga. That is the change I have experienced since the turn of the century, when I finished by doctoral study. I have come to understand the koloa in the people who act as fakaholofononga, for they have provided guidance, ofa and aroha for migrants, such as me, which makes our fononga pleasant and purposeful in Aotearoa New Zealand society.

Koloa in the Ngā Pae o te Māramatanga International Writing Retreat (IWR)

Koloa in Tongan language and culture is about the spirit of ofa, aroha: the good that is required by all relationships created during our fononga, be they spiritual, social, economic, philosophical and/or political. The koloa of retreats such as Ngā Pae o te Māramatanga IWR, lies in the value of 'ofa and poto, wisdom of the hearts of the participants. Such 'ofa and wisdoms ought to be reflected in their talanoa (dialogue) (Manu'atu, 2004), kōrerorero (Walker, 1990), writing, socialising, and application of the knowledges of their research in transforming the lives of the kaungāfononga (referring to the collective or the clan), their ways of being and practice.

At the retreats the discussions of themes that matter to Māori scholars were of great interest to me, such as kaupapa Māori research, excellence in Māori research, transforming Māori knowledge for economic benefits, Māori wisdom and Māori ethics. The discussions were good and ought to deepen Māori philosophy. Such in-depth discussions required energy, māfana and mālie (Manuʻatu, 2000), and wisdom from the spirit of God. Every scholar had a contribution to make from different standpoints, levels and depths, although not everyone was able to deepen their philosophical viewpoint. The inclusion of Māori language and culture in the intellectual discussion was a rare moment, and when that happened there was a different spirit in the air, the talk was intellectualising for the head and challenging to the heart from an ethical and moral standpoint. One of my Māori colleagues told me that what Tongan/Pasifika people could do to contribute to knowledge building in Aotearoa New Zealand society is provide māfana (warmth) and mālie (spirit, emotions) to intellectualising indigenous knowledges. I tend to agree with her, since a large majority of Tongan people are still very strong in Tongan language and culture, and many people still uphold their beliefs in God. The Kingdom's motto, "God and Tonga are my inheritance", is one that speaks about our Christianised faith. That is, the people's hearts must dwell in God's spirit, and that will secure an everlasting inheritance (Manuʻatu, 2014).

As an academic I might critique the ideas of everlasting inheritance and play out a mind-led exercise with no beliefs in the spirit. I might also unpack the koloa of the spirit in my heart and that provides the strengths of lotoʻofa (love), loto toʻa (courage), loto fakaʻamanaki (hope), loto maʻu (focus), loto melino (peace) and loto matala (openness), to name a few. The koloa of the spirit is, for me, all to do with our Tongan loto (wisdom of the heart).

In a way, the philosophical discussions that were generated in the IWRs over the years have contributed greatly to my thinking about the loto, the heart and the spiritual koloa therein, and much of my interest is in deepening my heart and thinking, to delve more into the wisdom of spirit. In my view, there was never sufficient talanoa, kōrerorero, about the spiritual knowledge and wisdom of Māori and Pacific people in any of the retreats. The quiet conversations—over a meal, on a walk, in the pool between colleagues and friends—accounted for much of the talanoa about these kinds of knowledge. Fakamālō atu ki he kaungā fononga mo pōtalanoa he ngaahi taʻu ʻo e IWR. My sincerest thanks to all of the participants from whom I learned about the koloa in each of you.

The work and writings of the late Emeritus Professor Ranginui Walker stand out for the energy, ideas, love and strength to speak clearly and strongly about the injustice to Māori society, over generations, and the wisdom of the Māori of Aotearoa. Knowing his wife, from teaching in the secondary school sector, as a person who loved the migrants from the Pacific Islands, I was not surprised that Deidre was the backbone of the family and a staunch supporter of Ranginui and his work. When I met Professor Walker I knew straight away that I was meeting a scholar, an academic, a leader, a critical thinker whose pen is powerful. His energy comes through in his book *Ka Whawhai Tonu Matou: Struggle Without End* (1990). A person who writes about whawhai tonu has perseverance, energy and a strong faith. I am privileged to have met, in my fononga, a great fakaholo-fononga like Professor Ranginui Walker.

In the IWRs I listened to the growing number of Māori academics from universities in New Zealand. In case I miss out anyone I do not want to list their names here, but I would like to thank Drs Mere Kēpa and Marilyn Brewin, who invited me to the halafononga of the IWR for many years. The thinking and writings of the participants in the IWRs have contributed to informing the education of Māori and Pacific peoples. As a Pacific migrant I value their works, ideas and writing as koloa, intangible, suitable to be upheld and deepened, for they pave the halafononga, pathways that value ourselves, our ancestors and our beliefs. Those who understand koloa will be filled with the spirit, and those who gather evidence will have so much to reinterpret and will come up with new analyses of education. The koloa are like arrows and bullets, the 'power of the pen' as in the reference to Professor Ranginui Walker: all work should benefit people, skilled and novices, peasants, oppressed and downtrodden. In other words, the power of the spirit, through their writings, aims to dispel despair and hopelessness in people caused by loss of land, values, language and culture. Like stars of the halafononga, words are prolific and clusters of them make impacts that last longer.

The IWRs have proven benefits for the participants, but I believe that the institutions will never be satisfied with the level of production by Māori and Pacific peoples, for obvious reasons. Perhaps the intangible koloa that I am talking about cannot be represented in writing, so we ought to come up with different ways of documenting and spreading knowledge and ways of applying such knowledge for the transformation of marginalised positions; and identify the spiritual, social, cultural and economic benefits of the knowledge transfer and application.

As a Tongan Pasifika, a space such as the interface of languages and cultures in the IWRs is energising, courageous, and hopeful. The ideas of Tongan academics such as the late Professor 'Ilaisa Futa Helu (Helu, 1999), the late Professor 'Epeli Hau'ofa (Hau'ofa, 2008), Professor Konai Helu-Thaman (Helu-Thaman, 1988) and Dr 'Ana Maui Taufe'ulungaki (Taufe'ulungaki, 2004) can be drawn together with the knowledge of indigenous Māori in a renewed spirit of 'ofa and aroha for God, King and country. This writing is speaking out loud from a spirit of hope and love for a much-refreshed set of values that brings creativity and ways of transforming our neighbourhood, our kaungāfononga, to value our struggles without end, where we understand the spirit with whom we connect and relate, and who returns us to the everlasting.

References

Bourdieu, P. (1977). *An outline of a theory of practice* (trans. R. Nice). Cambridge, UK: Cambridge University Press.

Hau'ofa, 'E. (2008). *We are the ocean: Selected works.* Honolulu, HI: University of Hawai'i Press.

Helu, I. F. (1999). *Critical essays: Cultural perspectives from the South Seas.* Canberra: Journal of Pacific History.

Helu-Thaman, K. H. (1988). *Ako and faiako: Educational concepts, cultural values, and teacher role perceptions in Tonga.* Unpublished doctoral thesis, University of the South Pacific.

Manu'atu, L. (2000). *Tuli ke ma'u hono ngaahi mālie: Pedagogical possibilities for Tongan students in New Zealand secondary schooling.* Unpublished doctoral thesis, University of Auckland.

Manu'atu, L. (2004). Talanoa malie: Innovative reform through social dialogue in New Zealand. *Cultural Survival Quarterly, 27*(4), 39–41.

Manu'atu, L. (2014). Tuli ke ma'u hono ngaahi mālie. In Kēpa, M., Manu'atu, L., & Pepe, M. (eds). *Booklet of poems. words & wisdom: The forum of indigenous thinkers, artists, poets, scholars and educators* (pp. 38–39). Auckland: Auckland University of Technology.

Manu'atu, L. (2016). Mālō e 'ofa!: Renewing the spirits of Tongan migrants through a new educational programme@the University. In L. Manu'atu & M. Kēpa (Eds.), *Ofa, alofa, aroha, aro'a love in Pasifika and indigenous education*. Berlin, Germany: Lambert Academic Publishing.

Taufe'ulungaki, 'A. M. (2004). *Fonua: Reclaiming Pacific communities in Aotearoa*. Paper presented at LotuMo'ui: Pacific Health Symposium Counties–Manukau District Health Board, Auckland.

Walker, R. (1990). *Ka whawhai tonu matou: Struggle without end*. Auckland: Penguin Books.

Chapter 8 Whakahihiko (inspirational, recharging): Dinayetr

Beth Leonard

Shageluk Tribe

Introduction

This essay begins with a self-introduction and summary of personal experiences in academic writing related to my dissertation journey. Following this I discuss my experiences of the 2010 International Indigenous Writing Retreat in Rotorua, influential indigenous scholars who have advocated for Alaska Native scholarship, and the ripple effects from the writing retreat model that continue to inspire and recharge indigenous scholarship and higher education programming in Alaska.

Introducing myself

I am Deg Xit'an (Dene'/Athabascan) and a member of the Shageluk Tribe of interior Alaska. In our language, Deg Xinag, the term 'dinayetr' has multiple meanings that connect with the intended themes of this chapter: 'inspirational' and 'recharging'. The literal translation of 'dinayetr' is 'our breath', an essential element in recharging the mind and body for work that lies ahead in our journeys. Other interpretations of this term include 'our belief system' and 'way/s of thinking', or processes that require continual inspiration and recharging, as the Deg Xit'an and other indigenous peoples seek to effectively negotiate within Western systems of education and governance. As demonstrated by indigenous peoples—Māori being one of the most successful examples in the global context—negotiation within these systems requires the development of a critical consciousness and mastery of discourses of power. Within higher education, academic writing remains challenging, especially for under-represented and marginalised students of colour, who have often been denied access to these discourses during their pre-higher-education experiences.

In 2007 I earned my PhD in Cross-Cultural Studies through the University of Alaska Fairbanks (UAF) Interdisciplinary Program. During the process of researching and writing my dissertation, which engaged with indigenous methodologies in the examination of Dene' oral traditions from my area, I looked to the work of one of my committee members, Dr Oscar Kawagley, the second Yup'ik scholar to earn a PhD. Dr Kawagley's insider research, previously unaccepted/unacceptable within Western academia, led to the internationally recognised publication *A Yupiaq Worldview: A Pathway to Ecology and Spirit* (1995). This book helped validate an insider research method and charted an early pathway for indigenous scholarship in Alaska.

Throughout my years as a graduate student, a number of mentors assisted with my academic writing. These scholars included Perry Gilmore, UAF professor emerita and currently professor of Teaching, Learning, and Sociocultural Studies at the University of Arizona, and Phyllis Fast, now University of Alaska Anchorage professor emerita. These mentors were particularly adept at pointing out strengths and weaknesses in my organisation and arguments in respectful ways that acknowledged the depth of my professional background and experiences. At that time, in my opinion, the dissertation writing process appeared to be a lone and lonely endeavour, as I was not familiar with the writing retreats in Aotearoa New Zealand, and the potential for creating long-term engagement with writing through the creation of a 'community of scholars'.

Rotorua, 2010

In 2007 I began a tenure-track position with the UAF School of Education. Early in 2010, as a 3rd-year, junior (non-tenured) faculty, I was making plans to attend the Ngā Pae o te Māramatanga 4th International Traditional Knowledge Conference in June of that year. Dr Bryan Brayboy, then serving as UAF President's Professor of Education, secured an invitation for me to attend the International Indigenous Writing Retreat in Rotorua following the conference. I had previously visited Aotearoa in 2004 for an International Research Institute conference at the University of Auckland organised by Dr Linda T. Smith, and had recently begun reading about the Māori scholarship-focused writing retreat model in Aotearoa. I was excited to have the opportunity to participate, observe the organisation of these retreats and consider similar opportunities and implications for Alaska Native faculty and students.

From the time the bus arrived at my Auckland hotel to transport participants to Rotorua and through the 5 days of writing and networking, other daily distractions/responsibilities (such as meal preparation and cleaning obligations) were non-existent. Scrumptious meals and snacks were served several times a day, with further opportunities for collegial interaction and networking. Much of the time was unstructured, except for mandatory sessions from 5:30 to 7pm each evening. During these sessions individual scholars presented their work and received feedback from the larger group. I presented an overview of my research in Alaska Native higher education and the Alaska Native Teacher Preparation Project (ANTPP), a US Department of Education grant-funded initiative then in progress at the UAF School of Education (2008–2012). This project supported 19 Alaska Native pre-service teachers to gain their education degrees and teacher certification, and included a cultural mentoring component in addition to financial and academic support. After the presentation, participants asked critical questions and offered valuable feedback that helped me reorient my perspectives on indigenous teacher preparation.

All of the participants had single rooms and we were free to structure our daytime schedules in ways that were most beneficial. Senior scholars offered a great deal of assistance to junior scholars and students, providing advice on dissertation writing, journal/book publications, and negotiating within higher education systems, including annual review and tenure processes for those in US institutions. The availability of senior scholars for question and answer sessions and one-on-one advising was particularly valuable, as regular appointments with mentors in university settings are often interrupted or under considerable time constraints due to the heavy workloads of many senior faculty. The relaxed atmosphere at the retreat, with an emphasis on developing collegial relationships, offered alternative approaches to what is often characterised in higher education as difficult dialogues. Although from diverse places, the participants were on the same page when engaging in conversations about decolonising methodologies in higher education for the purposes of promoting indigenous scholars and scholarship.

Considering the challenges of the ANTPP grant-funded project referred to above, including authentic inclusion of Alaska Native knowledge systems and pedagogies within the UAF School of Education curriculum at that time, I much appreciated the discussion with Dr Wally Penetito about his book *What's Māori about Māori Education?: The Struggle for a Meaningful Context* (2010). Struggles for meaningful context(s) are still challenging in Alaska Native and indigenous higher education today, but senior scholars such as Dr Penetito provide strategies for negotiating, inspiring and recharging transformation within higher education.

From my conversations with Dr Brewin (the retreat co-ordinator) and other participants, I learned that the purpose of International Indigenous Writing Retreats is to serve senior scholars, or junior scholars and PhD students—or any combination, depending on the needs at any particular time. The participants in this retreat included all faculty levels, including a group of PhD students from the University of Hawai'i-Mānoa. The time and space to reflect without interruptions (which is rare for those with family and faculty/student responsibilities), prepare a writing and research agenda and begin work on a current project were extremely valuable.

Dr Brewin arranged a visit to the Whakatane campus at Te Whare Wānanga o Awanuiārangi for the benefit of the international visitors. This break from writing was welcome, and the participants enjoyed the opportunity to engage with Drs Cheryl Stephens and Graham Smith on programme development at the tribal university. The participants valued the opportunity to observe self-determination and sovereignty in action within the whare wānanga. In my report to Drs Brayboy and Madsen on developing writing seminars and retreats, I recommended that we consider including 1- or 2-day trips or informational sessions for national or international guests who are invited to a UAF-sponsored writing retreat.

The writing retreat in Rotorua also facilitated a number of international networking opportunities for all participants. Following my presentation on ANTPP, Drs Linitā Manuʻatu (Auckland University of Technology) and Mere Kēpa (University of Auckland) invited me to participate as an affiliate investigator in a proposed project focusing on teacher preparation and the education of indigenous and migrant students in New Zealand. This was a wonderful opportunity to share knowledge on indigenous education and teacher preparation in an international context. I have since served as a reviewer for the *2013 Critiquing Pasifika Education Proceedings* edited by Drs Kēpa and Manuʻatu, and we continue to work together on various initiatives.

Indigenous places and spaces: The University of Alaska Fairbanks

Archaeological evidence places Deneʻ peoples in interior Alaska for approximately 12,000 to 15,000 years, although Deneʻ elders' commentary extends this period significantly. Preliminary recognition of University Hill as an indigenous space came after a 1994 speech by the late Chief Peter John, of Minto, Alaska. The former Director of Interior-Aleutians Campus, Clara Johnson, a now-retired Alaska Native scholar, administrator and activist in Alaska Native higher education, created posters of John's speech and these were published in 1998. Inclusion of this information in the academic catalogue followed 7 years later in 2001[1] and in 2013. Nineteen years later, the US Board of Geographic Names formally recognised Troth Yeddhaʻ, the hill now occupied by the University of Alaska Fairbanks.

The late traditional Chief Peter John of Tanana Chiefs Conference (a consortium of 42 Deneʻ tribal governments in interior Alaska) said that:

---

1 Retrieved from http://uaf.edu/catalog/current/overview/troth_yeddha.html

> Our people used to come to this hill to pick Troth ... Troth Yeddha'
> was important, a meeting place. The grandfathers used to come to
> talk and give advice to one another about what they were going to
> do. When they learned this place would be used for a school, the
> university, they came here one last time, to decide what they should
> do. They decided that the school would be good and would carry on
> a very similar traditional use of this hill—a place where good thinking
> and working together would happen ... They were also giving a
> blessing to their grandchildren who would be part of the new school.[2]

In describing the history of Troth Yeddha', the Chief John claims an
indigenous pedagogy of place, a hope that good thinking and working
together will continue, and that their grandchildren will be included
and appropriately served by this new school.

Over the past several decades indigenous and non-indigenous scholars at UAF have worked to promote access, success and good thinking
and working together within this indigenous space. The next section
discusses challenges and inequities in terms of Alaska Native student
numbers in comparison to Alaska Native faculty numbers. This is followed by a description of international networking and advocacy that
continue to contribute to the success of UAF's Indigenous Studies PhD
Program established in 2009.

Whakahihiko: Inspiring international networking

International networking for indigenous scholars is of critical importance, as indigenous faculty remain under-represented relative to the
numbers of indigenous students in many of our institutions. UAF has a
significant number of undergraduate Alaska Native / American Indian
students–19.6 percent as of Fall 2015.[3] However, Alaska Native/indig-
enous faculty membership has never exceeded 5 percent of the total
faculty. Faculty percentages are misleading, because there are several
different categories, including permanent (tenured) faculty, those eli-
gible for a permanent position (tenure track) and those under term/
temporary contracts (no long-term guarantee of employment). The level
of Alaska Native / American Indian graduate student enrolment is 8.6

---

2 Retrieved from http://archive.is/6gT0

3 Retrieved from http://www.uaf.edu/facts/

percent of 1,135 total students, or approximately 98 students. The total percentage presented in the university's demographic document does not separate graduate enrolment into master's and doctoral levels.

International networking has been critical in recent developments in Alaska Native higher education. In particular, the influence of Drs Graham Smith and Bryan Brayboy continues to inspire and recharge several initiatives. Dr Smith was the keynote speaker at the 2003 and 2010 Alaska Federation of Natives (AFN) Annual Convention (AFN is a statewide consortium of Alaska Native tribes). During this time he also acted as an advocate for indigenous education, and as advisor to faculty developing the UAF Indigenous Studies PhD Program. Drs Smith and Brayboy, currently University of Arizona Borderlands Professor of Indigenous Education and Justice, met with executive-level administrators in the University of Alaska system, along with key faculty and students, as advocates for the formation of an Indigenous studies PhD programme. During these meetings, Drs Brayboy and Smith utilised critical 'quantitative' methods in presenting their case to the former University of Alaska (UA) President, Mark Hamilton, that is, as of 2007, UAF had succeeded in graduating only four Alaska Native PhDs in the institution's 80-plus-year history of granting degrees (in 1970, 1998, 1999, and 2007). I recall their words to President Hamilton were, "we think you [the UA system] can do better."

Dr Smith also assisted in the design of the UAF Indigenous Studies PhD Program. In initial meetings, he encouraged us to consider a cohort model with a focus on transformational, applied research benefitting Alaska Native communities. Dr Smith also recommended a number of support activities for our PhD students and discussed the Māori writing retreat model, which seemed ideal considering that most scholars are seriously challenged by the amount of writing required to complete a dissertation, as well as by the number of journal articles and other scholarly writing required for promotion and tenure at US institutions.

In conjunction, often in collaboration with Dr Smith, Dr Brayboy continued his support of the students in the Indigenous Studies PhD and other graduate programmes at UAF. In addition to helping craft the ANTPP grant application (referred to above), he also drafted a successful application for funding from the Andrew W. Mellon Foundation for fellowships to support UAF PhD candidates during their dissertation-writing year. This grant was recently refunded through to 2020, as the Mellon Foundation is pleased with UAF's progress in developing Alaska Native PhDs. Although far from the '500 Māori PhDs' initiative already accomplished in Aotearoa, UAF will have awarded 14 Alaska Native/indigenous PhDs by May 2016, and we are grateful to Drs Brayboy and Smith for their mentorship during this process. The Indigenous Studies PhD Program would likely not exist in its current form, nor would this programme have been as successful, without their advocacy and leadership.

During his time as UAF President's Professor, Dr Brayboy developed and instructed several new graduate courses, including Critical Indigenous Research Methodologies, and Writing for Publication, a course designed to help graduate students develop an academic literature review aligned with dissertation standards.

> We are working on building a cohesive, coherent community of scholars in this course. To this end, it is imperative that you engage in the process of peer-review and learn to engage others' work in critical and constructive ways. (Brayboy, 2011, p. 3)

The writing course, offered twice as a 6-week summer course, met Monday through Friday as a 3-hour seminar, with the majority of class time reserved for writing, revising, peer and instructor review. Dr Brayboy described the development of a literature review as a daunting task and one of the more difficult aspects of a dissertation. He also clarified the development as a place where many emerging scholars struggle with situating their work. His use of metaphor in discussing the structure of writing generally—as "trying to capture three dimensions in two"—was useful as we worked on preparing dissertation chapters or journal articles during these intensive summer sessions.

Following the interest in and success of the Writing for Publication course, in 2012 Dr Brayboy, with the assistance of Dr Eric Madsen, then dean of the UAF School of Education, secured President's Professor funding to support a writing retreat at the University of Alaska Southeast in Juneau. The participants included UAF Indigenous Studies PhD students, Alaska Native faculty and UAF faculty of colour. Also participating were students from Arizona State University, Northwestern University, University of Oklahoma, the University of Hawai'i-Mānoa, and international faculty from Aotearoa, including the University of Waikato, Massey University and Victoria University of Wellington.

This 5-day event included morning and evening debrief sessions, shared meals at the campus cafeteria, and numerous comfortable spaces for writing individually or in groups. A beautiful glacier cruise served as the mid-week break and was much appreciated, especially by those from outside Alaska. Drs Bryan Brayboy, Linda T. Smith, Marilyn Brewin, Margie Maaka, Huia Jahnke, Wally Penetito and others served as senior scholar mentors to the group, often scheduling individual meetings with the students. The retreat also coincided with the release of the 2nd edition of Dr L. T. Smith's *Decolonizing Methodologies: Research and Indigenous Peoples* (2012), a publication that inspired many of us in Alaska to pursue further development of indigenous and indigenist models of research.

Whakahihiko (inspirational, recharging): Concluding comments

In the Deg Xinag language there is a term used in the pursuit of learning, 'getiy ngiłnath ts'i xiduxodinigianh', literally meaning 'I've been trying to learn for a long time'. Although the translation does not overtly refer to literacy, this concept and process of learning is concealed in the verb structure. Literacy is not a new endeavour within many indigenous cultures, but reading, writing and 'righting' the world using the English alphabet is a newer venture, as is negotiation within Western systems of higher education.

Developing systems to support PhD writing remains challenging, and rather than using a systemic approach, this responsibility is often left with the committee chair, with the remaining three committee members reviewing subsequent revisions recommended by the chair. In UAF's Indigenous Studies PhD Program, students progress through committee-approved coursework, then work through three written comprehensive exams consisting of a project overview, a literature review, and methodology. Once the (UAF Institutional Review Board-approved) research is completed, the dissertation writing begins.

Within our programme an on-site 'community of scholars' model is difficult as the current students hail from Alabama, California, Virginia, Washington, Guam and throughout the large state of Alaska. We concentrate on forming a distance cohort model through twice-yearly face-to-face and audio-conference PhD gatherings, tagged to the Alaska Federation of Natives annual meeting and other key conferences, such as the Alaska Native Studies Conference or the National Indian Education Association annual meeting. We often arrange for the PhD students to meet with the conference keynoters in separate sessions. Past presenters include Drs Graham Smith, Keiki Kawai'ae'a (University of Hawai'i-Hilo), Jo-Ann Archibald (University of British Columbia), and Marie Battiste (University of Saskatchewan).

We have not held a formal writing retreat since 2012. It is likely that this will require outside funding due to Alaska's current financial crisis. I would like to see these held as annual events due to many of our students' feelings of isolation during the dissertation-writing year. We do, however, continue to work among institutions with indigenous faculty (see Galla, Kawai'ae'a, & Nicholas, 2014), which diversifies the range of expertise available to students. Indigenous staff—too few, and heavily in demand for research and teaching networking collaborations—are critical factors in supporting junior faculty and pre-doctoral students and providing new learning opportunities for them.

The programmes and events described in this paper, largely inspired by the International Indigenous Writing Retreat, opened new, transformational possibilities for academic writing in "privileging the voices of Indigenous scholars and stakeholders" (McCarty, Borgoiakova, Gilmore, Lomawaima, & Romero, 2005, p. 4) rather than the often constrained parameters around what writing has to be or should be within the Western academy. Faculty and students in UAF's graduate programmes and I continue to be inspired by these opportunities to network, engage and recharge our academic writing within supportive contexts.

References

Brayboy, B. M. J. (2011). *Writing for publication* [course syllabus]. School of Education, University of Alaska Fairbanks, Fairbanks, AK.

Galla, C. K., Kawaiʻaeʻa, K., & Nicholas, S. E. (2014). Carrying the torch forward: Indigenous academics building capacity through an international collaborative model. *Canadian Journal of Native Education*, 37(1), 193–217.

Kawagley, A. O. (1995). *A Yupiaq worldview: A pathway to ecology and spirit.* Prospect Heights, IL: Waveland Press.

McCarty, T. L., Borgoiakova, T., Gilmore, P., Lomawaima, K. T., & Romero, M. E. (2005). Editors' introduction: Indigenous epistemologies and education: Self-determination, anthropology, and human rights. *Anthropology & Education Quarterly*, 36(1), 1–7. Retrieved from http://www.jstor.org/stable/3651305

Penetito, W. (2011). *What's Māori about Māori education?: The struggle for a meaningful context.* Wellington: Victoria University Press.

Smith, L. T. (2012). *Decolonizing methodologies: Research and indigenous peoples.* London, UK: Zed Books.

Chapter 9 Katakata o te ngākau: Humour and laughter among a community of scholars

Fiona Te Momo

Ngāti Pōrou, Ngāti Konohi and Ngāti Raukawa

Huia Jahnke

Ngāti Kahungunu, Ngāti Toa Rangatira, Ngāi Tahu, and Ngāti Hine

He ngākau tatū he oranga kata,
E hoa ma, ina te ora o te tangata.
(A contented soul, a life-giving laugh,
My friends, this is the essence of life.)

F. Te Momo and H. Jahnke

Abstract

For Māori scholars located in the academy, the principle of katakata is enacted every day as part of a cultural, social, political and psychological contract that enables spaces within institutions of higher education to be safe havens for our collective wellbeing. This is not unusual, because katakata, the spontaneous sounds and movements to express amusement and the ability to infuse humour in our daily lives, is common and fairly routine in Māori and indigenous communities in both formal and informal settings.

The notion of katakata as a source of wellbeing generally, and as it relates to Māori scholars in particular, remains an area that is largely unexplored. In 2015 and following a writing retreat for senior Māori researchers hosted by Ngā Pae o te Māramatanga, an opportunity arose to explore the principle of katakata as it relates to the Māori academic experience, which is a focus of this chapter. There is very little literature about the phenomena of indigenous laughter and humour—how the principle is exercised and applied in the lives of indigenous peoples. Yet, we would argue, katakata remains central to our wellbeing. From the limited writings on indigenous humour and laughter, a common theme is that colonised indigenous populations not only find comfort in sharing humour and laughter to endure difficult times, but in the process draw on unique ways in which humour is articulated in, for example, a community of scholars and their everyday lives.

Retreating to ponder, think, write and laugh

Katakata is at the heart of the work of Māori scholars in the academy. In 2015 a group of Māori academics descended on Taupō for a research retreat organised and funded by Ngā Pae o te Māramatanga. Over the course of a week the retreat became a safe haven to ponder, think, write and laugh. Each evening we gathered for dinner and over the course of a long, meandering meal we discussed politics, social issues and the many challenges we encounter in the academy. Meals became a precious time to unwind, to whakawhanaunga-tanga (socialise) and to katakata with great gusto. Reflecting on the nature of katakata and the profound effect that deep, side-splitting, belly-rumbling laughter has on our souls, Hone Morris best described katakata as follows:

> He ngākau tatū, he oranga kata, a contented soul, a life-giving
> laugh ... remembering the collegial sharing at Taupo and thought
> that probably best describes the feeling of being in a safe place
> academically with colleagues you trust which can in turn can free up
> the buttocks and allow a more convivial atmosphere to flow. (Hone
> Morris, pers. comm., 16 February 2016)

Faced with the possibility that this might be the last research retreat of its kind hosted by Ngā Pae o te Māramatanga, we decided to write about and reflect upon the uniqueness of our experiences. Since Māori humour is a significant outlet to soothe our souls and remedy our spirits, it seemed an obvious topic to explore. Most participants at the retreat were academics located in tertiary institutions, and all shared stories of their everyday workplace lives: the systemic institutional racism that served to bruise and batter our very souls while dealing with the multiple realities of what it means to be a Māori academic within the context of whānau. Recounting personal narratives in a humorous way aimed at drawing howls and tears of laughter from each other became an important source of unburdening, relieving, divesting and releasing the pain of everyday work stress while approximating some kind of work–life balance. The stress of dealing with the psychological contract whereby our institutions are meant to protect us from harm by providing safe environments was set aside during these hilarious episodes. Although laughter and Māori humour are normalised in te ao Māori, we found there was a dearth of literature on the topic. This chapter provides a small contribution to this most central characteristic of the human condition—Māori humour and laughter.

Katakata: Māori humour and laughter

According to Best (1920), the notion of Māori humour and laughter originates within the cosmological narratives. In one description, Best records Hinewhaitiri as a child of Thunder, whose thunderclap caused amusement in the heavens. In another, Hinewhaitiri is said to have produced a small clap of thunder because her mind was occupied elsewhere, which sent the sky children and other elements into a fit of laughter. A further version of this narrative suggests,

> Hinewhaitiri was distracted when it came for her turn to conjure up
> her loudest thunder clap. She was still thinking about the poor people
> below when she swung her large arms together and produced the
> weakest clap of thunder that had ever been heard. Everyone laughed
> at once, so much so that the hui could not continue. No one had the
> energy for any more destruction, they were too busy holding their
> sides and laughing. (Ministry of Education, 2016, p. 1)

The Hinewhaitiri narrative can be interpreted as portraying a slightly sinister aspect of laughter as a weapon against the weak. It can also suggest that it is okay to laugh with and at each other, even in the face of adversity and turmoil; that laughter can be a powerful weapon against destructive forces. The penchant for Māori humour to originate in contradiction (large arms producing the weakest thunder clap) is a familiar pattern, but it also demonstrates how laughter is harnessed to regulate social behaviour with joking and shaming tactics.

For Māori, humour is a part of any event or situation, including formal occasions. Whatever the situation or occasion, humour at its most powerful requires storytelling skills, exceptional timing, self-restraint, and knowing what is applicable and relevant and what is not. In other words, it involves having the skills and cultural intelligence to make explicit the boundaries of acceptable behaviour. During whaikōrero an eloquent speaker incorporates humour to gauge and engage the audience while delivering an important message. At less serious occasions the delivery of a comic element is not necessarily confined to the person delivering the whaikōrero, but can also include the people who support the kaikōrero with waiata. Salmon notes that this type of comic humour was recorded in the early 1800s:

> Sometimes the singers who accompany a speaker will provide the comic element. Kuia in particular were known to compose ruri (ditties) to comment humorously on proceedings in the marae. A military surgeon, John Savage, who visited the Bay of Islands in 1805, reported that the local people found some of their songs so hilarious 'as, in many instances, to occasion a total suspension of the performance, by the laughter of the audience'. (Salmond, 1997, p. 342)

An important institution in te ao Māori is the tangihanga, where humour is very often incorporated into oratory to farewell the dead. "At a tangihanga, while fare-welling a departed friend or relative, an orator may include a funny anecdote or good-humoured put down" (Salmon, 1997, p. 461). Māori humour is commonly shared amongst the whānau, iwi and hapū, and is "most likely to happen on the last evening of a tangihanga, when laughter and levity can enable the loosening of spiritual bonds with the tūpāpaku (deceased person) and enable the wairua (spirit of the deceased) to depart" (p. 461).

Holmes, Stubbes and Marra (2003) maintain that "Māori humour is fundamentally different from Pākehā" (p. 440). They argue that the difference is in the content, style and meaning, as well as what Māori find to be funny and how it is told. Humour "performs important cultural functions, such as enforcing social norms and expressing cultural identity" (p. 440). For Māori, humour and laughter indicate "awareness of, and even to draw attention to, their ethnic distinctiveness" (p. 441). In this context, humour and laughter can reinforce

> group norms and values by expressing in-group solidarity and making
> explicit the boundaries of acceptable behaviour. As a response to
> Pākehā hegemony, humour is a powerful strategy for subverting
> norms, deriding ethnocentric attitudes, and sending up 'proper'
> or 'correct' procedures. It is also a means of expressing the tension
> between roles. (Holmes et al., 1984, p. 441)

When Billy T. James and Prince Tui Teka soared to fame in the 1980s, they brought with them a contemporary form of Māori humour. Through their particular brand of comedy they both had the ability to cross cultural and racial boundaries that were sensitive to ordinary New Zealanders. Belich (2015) argues that

> the Māori comedian Billy T. James cleverly drew on old racist
> stereotypes about Māori, such as the Māori who was confused by
> the English language. By laughing at the stereotypes James helped to
> defuse them. (Belich, 2015, p. 1)

Billy T., although a great all-round entertainer, was an even better comedian. Most of his comedy centred on Māori people, but using various accents to great effect in his routines he also made fun of all nationalities. Billy T. was often accused, especially in the early days of his career, of stereotyping Māori. He didn't see it that way. His work was based on real-life observations of his family, friends and anyone else he happened across (Rotorua Travel Secrets, 2016, p. 1).

At the Ngā Pae retreat such real-life observations of family, friends and work colleagues, and the acting out of storylines including responses to Pākehā hegemony, were major features of our nightly storytelling anecdotes, especially by those speakers whose instinctive skills in the performance of a humorous tale were powerfully expressed in their antics and ability to communicate. In the process, such humour and the laughter that ensued provided deep expressions of cultural/tribal identity, group solidarity and long-lasting impressions that we carried to bed each night as delicious memories before sleep. It was not uncommon for these humorous tales to traverse variations on the themes of coping with academia while balancing the realities of home life, such as the vagaries of teenage angst, coping with ailing elderly parents, dealing with hyperactive mokopuna, surviving the aches and pains of getting old, contributing to iwi politics, and attending countless hui. A poem by the Reverend Mua Strickson-Pua celebrates the beauty that laughter and humour can provide for the human spirit:

> Prince Tui Teka, Billy T. James, Pio Turei, Gish; to the mokopunas …
> we share our laughter, humour, and comedy because we come from te
> moana nui a kiwa where Atua laughs at us and with us, never afraid
> of laughing loudly publicly because it is an emotion of being human
> to share freely, a blessing for creation and all of humanity. (Agee,
> McIntosh, Culbertson, & 'Ofa Makasiale, 2013, p. 71)

According to Derby (2013), for "much of the 20th century non-Māori New Zealanders maintained a comic tradition of the simple-minded but good-humoured Māori" (p. 1). He identifies Ngāti Porou as a tribe known for joking and playing the trickster, which they apply with great gusto to the unsuspecting, including Pākehā. Derby recounts how an elderly Ngāti Porou man tricked the local Pākehā store keeper by inventing a story and giving false information in order to gain monetary credit, supposedly on behalf of a 'work gang':

> The storekeeper was delighted to have such a lucrative order and a
> large bill was run up. The old man then gave his name as Kawehe-
> ite-rekareka, his address as Haere oti atu and his local marae as
> Waingaromia. When the storekeeper tried to send the bill, he
> discovered that Kawehe-ite-rekareka meant 'joyful parting', 'Haere
> oti atu' meant 'gone forever' and 'Waingaromia' meant 'out of sight'.
> (Derby, 2013, p. 1)

Derby[1] suggests that "for Māori much of the effectiveness of a good joke depends on how it is told" (p. 3), and that the laughter and joke are more than just the expressions of words but extend to the eyes, body

---

1 Quoting Biddle, personal comment, 2012.

language and an ability to communicate. This was certainly our experience at the retreat. One storyteller could provoke laughter with simple utterances and expressions in English with particular inflections that left us with little doubt about which tribe they were from. Yet another used their eyes and body language to communicate with such hilarious effect they barely had to speak at all and we fell about laughing. In these moments of sharing our stories in humour we experienced a level of collective solidarity and wellbeing we almost never experienced with Pākehā colleagues within institutional workplaces.

In a study of workplaces where there were high numbers of Māori employed, Derby compared Māori and non-Māori humour. The study found that Māori humour was essentially different from Pākehā humour, both in content and in style. Much emphasis in Māori humour is placed on the person's ability to deliver, their facial expressions, and the incorporation of mind, body and soul in order to engage their audience. In the words of a participant in the study, "our best speakers don't just tell a joke they become the joke" (Derby, 2013, p. 1).

What we experienced at the retreat was the particularity of Māori humour in the form of tongue-in-cheek figures of speech that served to make light of a situation, although the speaker may appear serious. Several stand-out figures of speech coined during the retreat became in-house jokes, the source of great hilarity and applied by various speakers at every opportunity, at which time they succeeded in 'becoming the joke'.

Reflecting on the effects laughter had on raising our sense of wellbeing at the retreat, it is not surprising to find that studies show that laughter and humour are attached to positive health benefits. Such benefits appear early, at birth, develop during infant stages, and are manifested in myriad language forms throughout childhood, through teenage years to adulthood. Laughter is an innate human behaviour, often triggered by culturally specific stimuli. Barnsley (1999) suggests that indigenous laughter occupies the space of cultural difference. Laughing at difficulties encountered in the lives of indigenous peoples, such as pain, poverty and/or oppression, does not erase life's challenges, but rather stimulates alternative and often more positive perspectives and points of view so that life's challenges appear less daunting and easier to cope with.

Some consider laughter to be a specific communication form of its own, what is referred to in the indigenous world as "native humour" (Andrews, 2000). According to Andrews, this particular brand of humour resides in all native peoples and "has traditionally been dismissed or ignored altogether" by non-indigenous people (Andrews, 2000, p. 10). Humour is an effective way for native people to express "the contradictions and dichotomies that shape the lives of Native populations today, as individuals and communities blend 'tribal tradition' and 'contemporary experience'" (Andrews, 2000, p. 3). Andrews maintains that native women writers

> have attempted to convey both the humanity of Native peoples
> and the pain that they have suffered over hundreds of years due to
> colonization and forced assimilation and acculturation. Humour can
> channel anger, celebrate survival, and even unite diverse groups of
> readers by bringing them together through laughter. Irony, in turn,
> often tempers the playful elements of humour by reminding readers
> of the legacy of oppression that has shaped the lives of Native North
> Americans for centuries; it also creates a space for other perspectives
> and voices, offering a venue for alternative articulations of selfhood
> and community. (Andrews, 2000, p. 3)

Similarly, in Australia Aboriginal people see humour as a way of coping with the difficulties they encounter in their homelands. Humour helps people to overcome obstacles, to make a situation lighter and enable them to conduct themselves in a customary manner. For example, if a person is meeting on 'Koori time', they can expect a lengthy wait for the meeting to commence.

> One of the key characteristics of Aboriginal people is their humour. No
> matter how dire the situation Aboriginal people are always able to find
> a humorous way of dealing with their life. 'When I looked around at all
> the carnage of our cultural abyss, I saw so much courage and so much
> laughter,' says Aboriginal film-maker Richard J. Frankland. 'One of the
> fundamentals of survival when life is knocking you about is laughter.'
> (Creative Spirits, 2016, p. 1)

The notion of humour as a coping strategy is the basis of Duncan's (2014) investigation into Aboriginal humour as a way to survive. Drawing on personal experience and understanding as well as historical accounts, Duncan's study recounts in detail "the onslaught of invasion, dispossession, powerlessness and oppression since the British invasion in 1788" (p. 1). The study found that despite the overwhelming challenges Aboriginal people faced, humour became a mechanism to overcome adversity, a strategy of hope and a catalyst to inspire them to continue living:

> The oppression of Aboriginal people following European settlement in Australia is marked by government policies which disempowered them, as well the racism which resulted in the clash of cultures and the crisis of identity for Aborigines … humour considers how far the emotions and humour are inextricably entwined, and addresses the elements of them. It is found that humour is a universal phenomenon but its manifestations vary from culture to culture. There is a close relationship between social structures and humour. Earlier anthropologists documented humour's capacity for easing social conflicts, relieving tensions and for promoting order, as they understood it. (Duncan, 2014, p. 1)

Expressions of humour are reflected in culture, especially when one group is oppressed by another, and where culture and humour transcend and adapt to the challenges of oppression. For the Aboriginal people of Australia, for example:

> It is shown how humour worked in particular settings as a complex institutionalised practice central to Aboriginal culture, and how and why it could be used to regulate social behaviour by joking and shaming tactics. Aboriginal humour had to change, expand or reform to meet new challenges. Humour was a weapon of the weak and it supported a subculture which grew out of the powerless situation in which Aborigines were placed by the dominant white group. Irony, satire and parody have been strategies of resistance in a colonised and a post-colonising Australia. (Duncan, 2014, p. 1)

Aboriginal humour evolved as a way to resist the dehumanising experiences of colonial terror that sought to silence and eradicate them in the process. Through various forums and mediums, Aboriginal humour is exercised, celebrated and actioned: "despite destructive European impact, it has persisted as a tool of survival, resistance, and the maintenance of identity" (Duncan, 2014, p. 1).

For Māori and indigenous peoples it is fair to say that laughter is linked to the notion of enjoying life despite our location (most often) within the lower socioeconomic substrata of society. Martinez explains,

> We grew up as the 'poorest' family on our block, probably neighborhood. However, if you asked me then, I wouldn't have identified myself that way. Our house is where all the neighborhood kids came to get fed, to hang out, to be a part of kindness and laughter. (Martinez, 2012, p. 2)

Martinez's indigenous roots stem from having a father who was of Apache genealogy and mother who was Pennsylvanian Dutch. The experience that is shared is not unfamiliar to an indigenous sensibility. We can all relate to those special spaces in our communities, the homes of our kin where as children we were fed and watered at any time of the day, chastised lovingly by our elders, and where laughter and kindness ruled. As Martinez suggests, "indigenous principles and beliefs of kindness and laughter are ritualized and practiced in specific customs" (p. 3). For Māori this is enacted within principles of whanaungatanga, tautoko and manaaki tangata. Humour and laughter in the Māori experience "are also practiced in less formalized commitments and expressions such as responses to admiration" (Martinez, 2012, p. 3) When applied to the workplace, humour can be transferred and utilised by academics as a pedagogical technique and as an effective way to administer pastoral care, where laughter becomes a way to provide support when completing tasks (Marsters, 2014).

For some indigenous communities, understanding indigenous humour is seen as an essential tool for community work. Others offer a caution by suggesting that putting native humour under the microscope changes its effects or impact, suggesting instead that one should avoid defining Aboriginal humour because

> if you haven't experienced it, you'll have to take it for granted—Indians, Inuit, Metis—they all love to laugh. Different tribes have different humour, but there are a couple of universal factors in Aboriginal humour: teasing and self-deprecation. (Crispin, 2014, p. 17)

The ability to express pleasure by laughing

In the broadest sense, katakata refers to the principle of expressing pleasure through laughing. In this community of scholars, katakata encompasses the physical, the emotions and the spirit; physical because to exercise humour demands that the scholars are not only effective story tellers but are able to tell the story through, with and by the whole body—the facial gestures of the eyes and eyebrows, the turn of the head, the movement of hands, arms and shoulders to give effect. Katakata physically involves a display of hilarity or disdain by altering movements of the muscles of the face, particularly the mouth. When katakata is effective, the stories will incite an uncontrollable roar or emotion of laughter. Importantly, of course, humour strengthens these scholars' survival and flourishing through complex difficulties in the academy.

By and large this community of Māori and indigenous scholars draws on humour and laughter, among ourselves and on a daily basis, in order to deal with the harsh realities of ignorance and racism that are reinforced through oppressive institutional structures and systems, as well as the acts of neglect and micro-aggressions perpetrated by colleagues. The fact that so many Māori and indigenous scholars remain in the academy is testament either to being beggars for punishment or to our fortitude.

For this community of scholars, humour is an important principle that sustains us in the face of adversity and difficult times. Katakata makes the unbearable more bearable and gives us a wonderful sensation of wellbeing. Put simply, for Māori and indigenous peoples in the university, katakata is a remedy—a strength for the body and soul in an otherwise toxic environment.

References

Agee, M., McIntosh, T., Culbertson, P., & 'Ofa Makasiale, C. (2013). *Pacific identities and well-being: Cross-cultural perspectives.* Dunedin: Otago University Press.

Andrews, J. (2000). In the belly of a laughing god: Reading humor and irony in the poetry of Joy Harjo. *American Indian Quarterly, 24*(2), 200.

Barnsley, P. (1999). Don Burnstick helps heal old wounds with laughter. *Windspeaker, 16*(11). Retrieved from http://www.ammsa.com/publications/windspeaker/don-burnstick-helps-heal-old-wounds-laughter-0#sthash.AVCNZFR1.dpuf.

Belich, J. (2015). European ideas about Māori: Modern racial stereotypes. *Te Ara—The Encyclopedia of New Zealand.* Retrieved from http://www. TeAra.govt.nz/en/video/29889/billy-t-james

Best, E. (1920). *The Maori genius for personification with illustrations of Maori mentality.* Wellington: New Zealand Institute.

Creative Spirits. (2016). *Aboriginal humour.* Retrieved from http://www.creativespirits.info/aboriginalculture/people/ aboriginal-humour#ixzz40qL4uCam.

Crispin, M. (2014). Reporting in Indigenous communities. Retrieved from http://www.stsailes.com/downloads/may-2014-newsletter.pdf.

Derby, M. (2013). Māori humour—te whakakata—Māori humour in the 20th century. *Te Ara—The Encyclopedia of New Zealand.* Retrieved from http://www.TeAra.govt.nz/en/maori-humour-te-whakakata/page-2.

Duncan, P. (2014). *The role of Aboriginal humour in cultural survival and resistance.* Unpublished doctoral thesis, University of Queensland, Brisbane.

Holmes, J., Stubbes, M., & Marra, M. (2003). Language, humour, and ethnic marking in NZ English. In C. Mair (Ed.), *The politics of English as a world language: New horizons in postcolonial cultural studies.* Amsterdam, The Netherlands: Rodopi.

Martinez, D. (2012). *Traditional kindness and ritual laughter.* Retrieved from https://www.culturalsurvival.org/news/ traditional-kindness-and-ritual-laughter.

Marsters, R. A. (2014, May). *Love, logic and laughter: Indigenous models of engagement with students and staff in tertiary education.* Paper presented at World Indigenous People's Conference, Hawai'i.

Ministry of Education. (2016). *Māori myths, legends, and contemporary stories.* Retrieved from http://eng.mataurangamaori.tki.org.nz/Support-materials/ Te-Reo-Maori/Maori-Myths-Legends-and-Contemporary-Stories/ Hinewhaitiri.

Rotorua Travel Secrets. (2016). *A glimpse into Māori humour.* Retrieved from http://www.rotorua-travel-secrets.com/maori-humour.html.

Salmond, A. (1997). *Between worlds: Early exchanges between Maori and European, 1771–1815.* Auckland: Viking.

Index

www.ingramcontent.com/pod-product-compliance
Lightning Source LLC
Chambersburg PA
CBHW080404270326
41927CB00015B/3349